INTERNATIONAL CRYPTIDS & LEGENDS

KENNEY W. IRISH

BEYOND THE FRAY

Publishing

BEYOND THE FRAY

Publishing

Contents

To my beautiful daughter, Hailey Belle

Acknowledgments

Thank you first to God.

Thank you to my best friend and wife, Selena Denise. Also, my best buddy, Little Man.

I would also like to thank these folks who have supported me in ways from just an encouraging word to other acts of support (in no particular order):

Michael Massey, Denis & Martha Chevalier, Chris Tebbetts, Ken Gerhard, Angel Vaow, E.R. Vernor, Gary Robusto, Luke Pullen, Edward Monge, Andrea Anesi & Kyle, Ted Van Son, Todd Campbell, Ron Yacovetti, Russell Acord, Doug Hajicek, Brian Johnston, Josh Turner & Family, Brian Todd, Cliff & Melissa Barackman, Ron Morehead, Ronald Murphy, Bryan Bowden, Adam Davies, Newell (Jay) Paire, Nicole Loiselle, Greg Samples, Howard Pitre, Damian Gray, Glen Ferguson, Shetan Noir, Steve Kulls, Daniela Agliolo, Paul Bestall, Bettina Moss, Jay A. Bachochin, Aleksandar Petakov, Al Santariga, Amy Bue, Stacy Brown, Anita Collier, Anna Maria Manalo, Barbara

Spoor, Barton Nunnelly, Bill Reap, Bob Pillsbury, Carter Buschardt, Chad Lewis, Charlie D. Perez, Darin Savard, Dean Bertram & Jenn, Eric Ogle, Glenn Harrison RIP, Greg Yost, Jake Dressel, Jason Hewlett, Peter Rean, Joedy Cook, John Kuykendall, Chuck Larson, Justin Decker, Kerry Carlson, Jerimiah Fountain & Family, Aunt Lisa, Michael Moran, Mike Anne, Mike Colontonio, Mike Luci, Archibald Franklin, Mike EC Whoop Patrick, Paul Bartholomew, Paul Kosco, Rick Fisher, Sam Shearon, Thomas Kardos, Tim Halloran, Timothy Morsch, Todd Neiss, Vincent Richardson, Lee Kirkland and Loren Coleman.

I would like to thank these organizations (in no particular order):

All Beyond the Fray authors; the New York Bigfoot Society; Tri-City NY Paranormal; Bigfoot Quest Radio; the Rochester Para-Fest; *Coast to Coast AM* with George Noory; *Beacon of Light Radio* show; *Storming the Unknown* podcast; Champ Day-The Lake Champlain Monster Festival; NYS Writers Institute; Bear Pond Books; Sasquatch Festival Whitehall, New York; Cryptid Con; Smokey Mountain Bigfoot Festival; Dogman and Cryptid Conference; Michigan Bigfoot Conference; Dead Con; *Haunted Hospitals*; Travel Channel; Discovery Plus; CARC; *3 Beards Podcast*; the Paranormal Network; *Nite Callers Bigfoot Radio*; *Open Minds Podcast*; *Squatch GQ* magazine; Squatch 'n Indiana; The International Cryptozoology Musuem, Portland Maine; North American Bigfoot Center, Boring OR.

Anyone or any organization not named, you are loved and appreciated!

Foreword

JOSH TURNER, THE HOST OF PARANORMAL
ROUND TABLE PODCAST

I was introduced to Kenney W. Irish when he reached out to me to talk about the paranormal and cryptids in particular, an interest we have in common. I enjoyed our conversations so much, I have kept in contact with him ever since. Kenney is a great guy and very down to earth. I consider him a good friend who is very knowledgeable in the field of cryptozoology, a subject that is near and dear to me.

In Kenney's latest work, we are presented with a selection of cryptids. Some that you may be familiar with, but others that may be new to you. What fascinates me the most is the collection of cryptids from so many different countries. Kenney has captured a great amount of information regarding these cryptids and the legends surrounding them. The painstaking research he has done on the subject matter comes through in the attention to detail presented in each chapter. I can only imagine the amount of patience and fortitude it took to put this all together.

I have spent most of my life delving into the subjects found in this book, as well as many others after my own personal encounter with a creature commonly known as Dogman, when I was a teenager, in my hometown in Texas. Since then, the subject of cryptids has become a lifelong passion. I have read countless books about these legends and have interviewed many people regarding their personal encounters.

I am excited to say he has done a great job relaying the information regarding these legends of cryptids to you, the reader. I am confident that you will enjoy all the information he has captured in this book as much as I have.

Russia

Today, Russia, whose capital is Moscow, is known as one of the largest countries on the globe. As of 2021 the population is 144.5 million. It spans eleven time zones across two continents, Asia and Europe, and has coasts on the Pacific, Atlantic, and Arctic oceans. The earliest to step foot in Russia was around AD 500. These settlers, along with Slavs from the west, came together and built what is called a fortress that would over time become the Ukrainian city of Kiev.

Kiev developed into a powerful empire that ruled European Russia for more than two hundred years, then separated into Belarus, Ukraine, and Muscovy. Muscovy's capital is Moscow. In the thirteenth century, Mongol invaded in the south, which drove people to settle in Moscow.

In the mid-1550s, Ivan IV, a Muscovite ruler, became Russia's first tsar after he overtook and drove the Mongols out of Kiev. In the year 1682, Peter the Great at the age of only ten became tsar and for forty-two years worked to make Russia more modern and more European. In the year 1917, the Russian government pushed out the tsar and, in return, formed an elected government. Shortly after the tsar was overthrown, Vladimir Lenin created the Union of Soviet Socialist Republics, also known as the USSR.

The USSR teamed up with the United States in World War II. Shortly after the war in 1945, the two nations' relations became strained, as both wanted to be the superpower. This all led up to the Cold War, which ended in 1991 when the Soviet Union dispersed.

Eighty percent of Russians' ancestry can be traced back to the Slavs who moved in and settled in the country approximately 1,500 years ago. Russia is a federation of eighty-six republics, territories, districts, and provinces. All the territories are controlled by the government in Moscow. The head of state is a president elected by the people.

Russian Yeti

Described as a large bipedal creature dwelling in cold areas and hard-to-reach territories of Russia. One such creature is known as "Menk, or "hairy forest giant." The creature was given this name by the Mansi, the indigenous people of the area. Mansi, formerly called Vogul, western Siberian peoples, can be found living in the Ob River basin area in central Russia territory. They speak what is called an "Ob-Ugric" language of the "Finno-Ugric."

The creature is described as tall, standing in the range of nine feet in height, covered with dark fur, and extremely strong. Many Mansi tribespeople have described an unusual whistling type of sound made by the creature when encountered. It's said Menk hunts deer and other animals in the area, such as bear, for nutrition.

Menk is also suspect in one of the most bizarre and still to this day unsolved mysteries, "the Dyaltov Pass Incident." On the night of February 2, 1959, in the area of the Ural Mountains also known to the Mansi tribespeople as "the Mountain of the Dead," nine students at the Ural Polytechnic Institute, now known as Ural Federal University, met a gruesome and unexplainable fate.

The group headed out in January, led by Igor Dyaltov. They had packed up and set out on a hiking trip to the Ural Mountains, with a target location of the Otorten Mountain. This hike would fall under a category three hike, which means they would come across sections of rugged terrain, large rocks, steep and shallow slopes. All the students were experienced hikers and skiers. This journey would bring its challenges, but nothing the experienced Russian students couldn't handle. It's said on the night of the mysterious incident, they were only about six or seven miles from their expected and well-planned-out location. It's said when the students stopped communicating and did not arrive back by the expected return date, search parties were deployed.

When the first search party arrived, which is believed to be around three weeks after the tragedy, they found abandoned tents with much of their gear inside. Some of the items found consisted of boots, gloves, jackets, and tools. This was very odd considering these items could have been used by the hikers to help them survive. Strangely, there appeared to be deliberate cuts in their tents, which are believed and determined to have been made from the inside. Some say it was to be able to see outside from different angles. The tent doors were still zipped shut.

When their bodies were discovered, their gruesome

and mangled injuries left all baffled and in complete shock. Many were unclothed, in strange and unusual positions and locations. It's said some had crushed skulls, some were missing eyes, while another was missing her tongue. Others were struck by a force comparable to that of a speeding car colliding with a human body. The Russian government quickly closed the case. They gave an explanation stating the hikers died of hypothermia, and that it was most likely an avalanche that caused the gruesome and repulsive scene.

There are many theories to date, such as UFOs were involved, with the claim of orbs and strange lights in the night sky seen in photos taken by the students. There were also traces of radiation at the site. Some speculate that the Mansi tribespeople were to blame. A Russian missile testing, or even a low wind pattern that generates a low-frequency infrasonic sound that is so unpleasant, some speculate that a few of the hikers could have been so affected by the unpleasant and irritating sound that they were pushed to a breaking point of insanity.

The one theory that many believe, especially in the subject of cryptozoology, is Menk, the Russian yeti, is to blame. There was a picture taken of a dark lurking figure that could in fact be one of the hikers, but to this day has never been 100% confirmed. It has been said by some that when the search party arrived at the location, there were in fact large nonhuman footprints discovered at the site of the incident.

So according to this theory, the group had been viciously attacked by the Russian yeti. A violent such animal attack could explain many of the injuries and could explain the reason the group cut open and ran from their tents, leaving behind warm clothing and items that would help them survive the extreme conditions of the location.

The Leshy

The Leshy is what many call a masculine woodland-type spirit. A forest monster that lives to protect and kill. The entity is said to watch over and protect the animals and forests of which it dwells. Some refer to the Leshy as a forest witch or a warlock. It's believed that different forest territories will contain a Leshy, while others believe there is only one that covers all and fiercely protects the territory from other spirit entities. The folklore also speaks of a Leshy having a wife and even having children at one point.

A Leshy usually appears as a large humanoid-shaped man. His eyes are green, and he has a long thick beard, and his hair is said to be made up of vines, sticks, and dirt. He is also described as having a long tail, hooves for feet, and horns protruding from the sides of his head. Some descriptions claim parts of the Leshy are treelike, with long thick branches and/or roots. The roots can be used to steady the entity crea-ture to the ground in battle, but are also used to catch, whip, slice, and strangle wanderers who disrespect the forest land. It's believed he has the ability to change in size. From a large, towering tree to as small as a cricket.

He is believed to carry a large hammer-type club to show dominance. Considered a spirit, it has physical and earthly traits. For example, he can bleed as a human would, and it's said the blood runs the color of blue. Legend states he can cast no shadow, but can shapeshift or transform himself into many unusual and bizarre forms, from a tree to plants and even a gray wolf. It's said that the Leshy has a spiritual bond with the gray wolves of the territory. It's often been witnessed in the company of wolves and even bears by those who have had a chance encounter with the entity, and those who came across and upset the Leshy but lived to tell the tale.

The Leshy is also believed to be able to infect humans with disease, sickness, and even death. This is said to be one kind of an attack on humans who disrupt the forest in which he dwells. He is said to have the ability to imitate voices of people familiar to wanderers and lure them into caves, where the individual will be tortured with such methods as tickling and using wooden clubs to beat the people to death, and sharp rocks to slice open wanderers and any evil-doers who dare disrespect and trespass in the forest territory of the Leshy.

Some refer to the Leshy spirit as a good entity, while others a demon. It's believed to be evil by many. Some say they enjoy kidnapping young children and women. The Leshy has been suspect in many unexplained abductions and missing people who entered the forest land of the Leshy and were never seen or heard from again.

It is believed one can become friends with a Leshy, and the Leshy, once full trust is established, will offer to teach the human the secrets of their mysterious magic and powers. It's said that shepherds and farmers would seek friendship pacts with the Leshy and offer gifts to them; in return the Leshy would protect their livestock and farmland.

The Leshy despises those who disturb the forest by cutting down trees instead of using the timber of already fallen trees and branches on the ground from recent storms. The Leshy is said to use the axe of the individual to chop off their limbs so they feel the same agony of the timber they so carelessly and without remorse hacked at. They are also known to have thrown large branches and boulders at those who dare perform such an act.

If one is to take a tree in the territory of a Leshy, they are to first seek approval from the spirit guardian, offer a gift to the forest, such as helping guard the territory, and if at that point full approval is granted, they will be allowed to use their axe to take down a tree. The selected tree must first be shown to the Leshy for ultimate approval. If final approval hasn't been granted and the individual swings at a tree, the Leshy has been said to take the axe and hide it, and cast disease or a curse onto the person and their family. It's also believed that the Leshy will use the axe to murder the person, then move on to the family of the individual for disobeying or not following the strict guidelines.

Baba Yaga

Baba Yaga is said to be a mythological witch in Slavic legend. Baba Yaga is a supernatural spirit being, but lives in many ways as a flesh and blood forest witch.

Her appearance can be described as an elderly old woman. To some she has been seen as just a little old grandmother-type figure, while others describe a horrific and grotesque appearance that once witnessed, you can never unsee.

Some describe her appearance as having a facial deformation. One characteristic would be she has a set of iron teeth, which appear when she grins under her long and crooked nose. Seen as thin and incredibly emaciated, she is usually witnessed hunched over.

Legend tells us that Baba Yaga lives in a house-like cottage standing on just chicken legs known as an "izbushka," a traditional wooden home in the Slavic region. It is believed that the house can actually move around on these legs, being seen in different territories. The front door's keyhole is said to contain sharp razor-blade-type edges, as to protect the home from intruders. Surrounding the home is what can only be described as a fence of death and dismay. The fence is made up of human bones, both children and adult. The skulls of the victims have a candle placed in each one as a way of setting an eerie lighting to the property and sending a message of warning and certain doom to anyone who may wish to trespass onto the property.

Some Russian legend believes that Baba Yaga doesn't live alone, but has three sisters just as hideous and in many ways more disturbing in appearance. They all have an unsatisfiable appetite, and it's believed they feast upon human flesh. This includes children and adults. There is a large oven and a large cauldron-type pot that is always boiling, and the water is stirred with the bones from past meals.

Baba Yaga is said to be transported around by sitting in a large hovering mortar that is controlled and directed with a large pestle, which is said to be used as a method of steering, like a rudder on a ship. Baba Yaga will use this device to chase innocent children and adults through the Russian forest, capturing them and returning home to feed upon the victim's flesh with her three sisters. Russian folklore speaks of the family to be cannibalistic monsters and/or supernatural witches.

Folks who have encountered Baba Yaga and lived to tell the tale claim the attack is vicious in nature. They first hear a screeching that is so intense that for some, it stuns the human body, and all muscles seem to cramp, and the individual will fall to the ground. They will try to crawl into hollow logs and holes to escape. Others claim that there is a wretched odor first experienced, which is believed to be permeating off the witch's body. It's described to be so putrid smelling, one's eyes will water, making it hard for them to see to escape, and it burns the nose. Also, many vomit immediately after the odor is detected.

———

The Vodyanoi

The Vodyanoi is a creature said to have origins in Slavic mythology and legend. Some refer to the creature as the "water spirit" or "water entity." It is said to be a spirit by some, while others claim flesh and blood. They are said to look like merman and/or siren-type creatures. Described to have black scales with a green tint, a fish tail, fins, and hair that resembles such sea plant life as seaweed. Some describe the creature as having a frog-like face with protruding warts covering the body.

Found in an assortment of water such as oceans, rivers, lakes, and even in dense and murky swamps. Said to be nocturnal and only appearing at night. During the daylight hours, he can be found at the bottom of the deepest bodies of water. Legend states mermaids and mermen are considered to be the children to the Vodyanoi. The creature is said to be male and the king of the aquatic beings that inhabit the seas and bodies of water. They are to be respected and even feared. Many believe the Vodyanoi to have a wife and sometimes multiple wives.

The Vodyanoi is said to have the ability to change in appearance, or to "shapeshift," whenever desired for certain purposes. Some such changes would be the ability to resemble a floating log, a fish, and even a large frog. They are said to be immortal but do age, as a human would. In the water they have great strength but are said to be weak and feeble on land. Some believe it's due to leaving wet footprints and puddles on land, thus draining the creature of energy and strength.

It is believed if you come across a Vodyanoi, there is a good chance you will be abducted and taken to the deep depths of the waters to be first drowned and then consumed. It's suggested to wear a crucifix before approaching any bodies of water. It's believed it will keep the creature at bay, as its evil side cannot penetrate the significance of the meaning behind the cross. It is also said to avoid bodies of water when at all possible. One who follows the safety warnings will be safe.

Many human carcasses that wash up on the shores of oceans, lakes, and riverbanks in many cases are seen and written off as some type of aquatic attack by the known and common water predators in the area, or a victim of a drowning. While others suggest and warn that it's the work of the evil water spirit Vodyanoi. Some bodies retrieved have had strange and unidentifiable markings, or what some might call bite marks, that appear to have human characteristics. While there is no way to 100% substantiate these claims, there are enough individuals who believe, and in their minds know, these attacks are, in fact, the work of the Vodyanoi water entity.

The Domovoi

The Domovoi is believed to be what is referred to as a "house spirit" in Slavic mythology. "Domovoi" comes from the Slavic word "dom," which translates to "home." An entity or being said to be of good and not evil who dwells and finds refuge in Slavic homes and most commonly can be found sitting behind the home's stove. It's believed the Domovoi protects the family from harm, such as fires, floods, lightning strikes and even intruders/trespassers. If misfortune to the family is pending, the Domovoi warns them by making knocking sounds on the walls and ceilings.

However, if it becomes upset and feels disrespected or unappreciated, the spirit is known to act up, playing tricks on the humans, such as creating trip hazards or hiding tools. In some cases, causing damage to parts of the home. Some damages believed to be caused by the Domovoi consist of broken windows, furniture, and random holes in the walls. The Domovoi must be given gifts such as leftover food. Small cloaks are appreciated, which gives them something to wear.

The Domovoi is often called the "master" of the house. Eastern Slavs still say every household has its own spirit-type guardian, which is believed determines and oversees the well-being of all family members, their health, crops, and livestock. Described as masculine in body type, but extremely small, with a tail, tiny horns, a long beard, and with a body completely covered in dark coarse hair. According to some traditions, the being has the ability to take on the appearance of an old man, woman, a cat, and even a pig. Other versions describe the Domovoi as having a wrinkled and drooping face, gray hair, gray beard, and green glowing pulsating eyes.

In some cases, the Domovoi is never seen by the adults of the family who live in the home, but only by the children. The creature will most commonly make its presence known and reveal itself in such ways as initiating odd noises, a murmuring or chattering vocal, or the sound of footsteps in a room.

He only comes out at night when the house is quiet and all are asleep. When all are asleep, he visits all the family members one by one and caresses their hair and glides the palm of his hands across their faces with an intent of protection and good health. The Domovoi never leaves the family he has adopted. If the family moves to another place or builds a new home, he will follow.

Oddly enough, if there is no male figure present in the household, and the head of the house is a woman, the Domovoi strangely enough is said to become a woman spirit.

2

Malaysia

The first known Malay kingdoms appeared around the year AD 200. The first people to live in Malaysia were Stone Age hunters and gatherers. Stone Age farmers arrived in the territory of Malaysia and dominated, pushing the Stone Age hunter-gatherers to the outskirts and remote areas. The farmers practiced what was called "slash and burn agriculture." Slash and burn was the practice of clearing a territory by burning areas of the rain forest. The farmers would then use the land to grow their crops. It is said, after a few years, the land would become exhausted, and the farmers would clear a new area. However, within a few years, the previous area would become covered in vegetation and would become fertile and ready to use once again.

During World War II, Malaysia was occupied by

the Japanese from 1941 to 1945. Fast-forward to February 1, 1948, and the Federation of Malaysia was formed. In 1955 the Reid Commission was formed to prepare a constitution for Malaysia, and it achieved its independence on August 31 in the year 1957. As of this day, Malaysia is a prosperous and growing country. It has an approximate population of thirty-two million. Malaysia's capital, Kuala Lumpur, is located on the west side of Peninsular Malaysia, closer to the Indonesian island of Sumatra. The country of Malaysia is two separate areas of land known as Peninsular Malaysia and East Malaysia. The two regions are separated by the South China Sea, by approximately four hundred miles. Combined, they'd be roughly the size of the state of New Mexico.

East Malaysia is home to Mount Kinabalu, the country's highest point, which has an elevation of 13,455 feet. Malaysia shares borders with Thailand to the north and Indonesia and the island of Singapore to the south. Singapore is separated from Malaysia by a bridge.

Most of the country's population lives in Peninsular Malaysia. The four main ethnic groups in Peninsular Malaysia are the Malays, who make up about half the population; the Chinese; the Orang Asli, an indigenous or native group in Southeast Asia; and South Asians with roots in the countries of India, Pakistan, and Sri Lanka. Many of these groups live in East Malaysia. East Malaysia is also home to other indigenous groups, including the Iban, the Bajau, and the Kadazan.

The Bès

These spirits are said to be evil and of the Jah Hut, an Orang Asli people from peninsular Malaysia. The "Bès," also known as "Hantu," are associated with human sickness and disease. Sickness is caused by the influence and presence of the Bès. It's said by night, while one is asleep, their soul exits their body and will wander. Legend states if a Bès comes across a wandering soul, it will capture it and will prevent it from returning to the owner of the soul. The body will then fall incredibly ill and, in most cases, will not survive.

Healing can only come by the way of Puyang, or by the powers of a medicine man. It is believed they can locate a missing or abducted soul and, with the assistance of good spirits and angels, return the soul to the body it belongs to.

Wood carvings of the Bès have been created for visual effect on how they would appear, so all will know and have an understanding of how they look in case some poor wanderer crosses paths with one.

Bès Pa'

The Spirit Pa' is said to be found in and around rivers and other certain bodies of water. It's said to resemble a jellyfish, which is why it's also referred to as a "jellyfish" spirit. As one would want to avoid a natural jellyfish, seeing one wouldn't necessarily send one running, but more of a state of mind to stay away. With this spirit, even coming in close contact could result in an overtaking or possession. Many believe the spirit will bury themselves in mud, which is used as a form of camouflage. Anyone who steps upon a buried pa' in the mud will be abducted and pulled down into the mud along with the spirit, never to be seen again.

Many unexplained disappearances of those who were known to be heading to bodies of water but were never seen again are believed to have fallen victim to the spirit. Some say to avoid such a fate, one must carry a mixture of crushed iron rust, along with broken glass, and spread it all over the area or territory by the water in all visually muddy areas.

The spirit is believed to be able to attach itself,

taking over the human's natural ability to breathe and think. The spirit will then slowly drain the victim's energy as it eats away and devours their soul.

The unfortunate act of the spirit attaching and draining one's soul to depletion means the individual will be walking and wandering aimlessly possessed until all energy has been devoured. There have been many witnesses to such a person whose soul and body has been inhabited by the Spirit Pa' entity. The unlucky individual looks to be in some form of trance, looking straight ahead and oblivious to their surroundings. While others are said to be yelling in an unrecognizable language, arms flailing while foaming at the mouth. They at times will chase after and attack anyone unlucky enough to be in their presence.

While some have had rocks thrown at them by the possessed, others have been viciously ravaged by being scratched, thrown to the ground, or beaten. The possessed can become cannibalistic in nature and even attempt to devour and consume the poor individual who has crossed its path.

The Bès Jě'la Kòy

The Jě'la Kòy, also known as the "spiky-head spirit," is another of the Bès or spirits originating from legend and folklore of the Malaysia people of Jah Hut. It is said to be found and lives upon the top of termite hills. By no means seen as an evil spirit, it does in fact have an ability that is seen by the believers as dark. It is believed the Bès Jě'la Kòy can determine and predict how long a certain individual's life span will be.

If one comes across the spirit, it's believed their time of walking the earth is coming to an end. Some see encountering the entity as a blessing. They will start to get their business in order, as they believe they are about to pass on and also become a spirit. If the spirit concludes that a person's lifespan is to be cut short, it will take their spirit immediately into a termite hill to dwell for eternity. For what purpose? That question has yet to be answered. It's written and spoken into belief that the spiky-head spirit takes one person a year into its termite hill based on the individual's life coming to an end prematurely, or what is to be "before their time."

Many young adults and children who have disappeared are believed to have been taken by the Bès Jě'la Kòy. While some find comfort in that belief that their loved one is being protected, others are angered and curse the spirit, believing the spirit to have taken the soul of the individual for its own pleasures, while others believe for consumption, draining the energy of its human soul.

The Bès Dangon

The Dangon, "buttock spirit," is also a spirit from legend and folklore of the Jah Hut people of Malaysia. Not much information on this spirit, but it's said to dwell and take refuge upon the very top of coconut trees. Anyone who dares to attempt to climb the tree will be met with an invisible force or impact that will knock the poor soul to the ground. As a spirit, one would have a hard time understanding how there are claims that the spirit can in fact urinate and produces humanlike stool.

The spirit is said to completely cover the entire tree with urine and stool, which in return kills the coconut tree, so it can no longer produce for any humans and will perish.

Bès Chèm

The Chèm, a "bird spirit," is said to be associated with a multitude of Malaysian evil entities and/or spirits. This is another spirit entity said to live in trees only with large branches and has earthly types of behavior that will result in the physical. This bird spirit is said to urinate upon unsuspecting persons who may be passing by the tree branch they are perched upon. Once the urine has covered the individual, the spirit bird will then release and cover the urine-soaked person with feathers. These feathers are described as tiny and believed by some to be poisonous, and if not removed immediately, the unlucky and unwilling participant could die.

There are many reasons believed by some regarding why the spirit bird follows this strange ritual. Some say to be chosen is a sign of greatness, while others believe it's a bad omen and means sickness will soon fall upon the individual and their family members. Another unusual and strange belief is that the person who experiences the urine and feathers will become thin forever. Why? Well, at this time I have found nothing that explains this belief.

The bird spirits are also said to make unusual noises, not such a vocal that one would expect from a bird. But then again, these are spirit birds. Some say they make an "O-O-O" sound, and some sound like they are saying "POK-POK-POK." It's believed that they all have similar characteristics. Some actually have the ability to cause someone to become nauseous, followed by a severe headache. Others believe the bird spirits hold the ability to possess children and cause convulsions, while others say they can completely steal one's soul.

———

Bès Rap

The Rap, known as the "pig spirit," is another spirit Bès originating via the folklore and legend of the Jah Hut people of Malaysia. It is believed to dwell in the deep hard-to-reach territories of the jungle. They are usually found near a fig type of tree called the "pokok ara."

They are extremely territorial when it comes to this tree. If anyone approaches and attempts to remove fruit from the tree, the spirit pig will attack, chasing off the wood-be intruder or, as they see it, thief. If the individual is able to get away, if any of the spirit's saliva, which is said to foam and drip from the creature's mouth, makes contact with the human, they too will foam from the mouth and become extremely sick, and death can occur. There is also a belief that the person can become possessed by the spirit.

The pig spirit is said to be able to produce stool, or

droppings, that produce an unusual amount of heat and release an odor that is so nauseating to humans they will immediately vomit. Very much like the saliva, any contact with the spirit pig's feces will result in one becoming extremely sick, and could even result in death.

———

Bès Kotak

The Kotak, a "box spirit," is another Bès, or spirit, from the folklore and legend of the Jah Hut people of Malaysia. It is described as appearing much like a box. The spirit can be found dwelling by riverbanks, much like the Spirit Pa', hiding in the mud. Some also refer to the entity as a river spirit.

It is believed the spirit is extremely evil in nature, and anyone who enters the river is in great danger of being possessed by the spirit. It's said that the spirit will grab ahold of a person and sit or lie across their chest, holding them under the water. The person's body will feel extremely heavy, and they will not be able to move their limbs to swim or defend themselves. The spirit will dominate, pushing them down and burying them in the river's mud.

It is said that after the death of the individual, the

spirit will hold the body in the deep mud of the river for up to a week. The spirit will then release the body, which will float to the surface of the water to be discovered by passersby. It is warned by legend to stay out of the water and watch where you step when approaching the river.

The Orang Dalam

The Orang Dalam is a beast that is said to roam the jungle of Johor in Malaysia. The creature is said to resemble what some refer to as a Sasquatch, or Bigfoot. The Orang stands and walks bipedally, and witnesses claim its height is in the eight-to- ten-foot-tall range. The body is said to be fully covered with black fur-like hair, and due to the high temperature and climate, it has a terrible odor that can be detected long before the creature gets close to any humans.

The creature is said to feed on fruits, fish, snakes, and any other type of nutrition it catches. Some believe that humans who have mysteriously disappeared have fallen victim to the creature, having been abducted and consumed.

The local residents, the Orang Asli people, are first-hand witnesses to the creature. They have had many face-to-face encounters with the beast. They refer to the Orang Dalam as "Hantu Jarang Gigi." This name translates as "snaggle tooth," or "snaggle-tooth ghost." In legend, some believe the creature to be a spirit of a demon, while others speculate or believe the creature may be a surviving member of *Gigantopithecus*.

3

China

The earliest archeological records date back to the Shang Dynasty. Chinese history is divided into dynasties; each reflects a period of when a line of emperors ruled the territory. The first recorded empire was the Qin dynasty, which began and dates back to 221 BC. The last emperor was overthrown in the year 1912, allowing China to become a republic.

For centuries, China was ahead of other countries in many subjects such as math, science, and certain technologies. The Chinese invented paper and were the first to use paper money. The first type of paper money was called "Jiaozi." It was first printed in the year 1023. They can also be credited with the creation of printing, silk fabrics, and gunpowder, to name a few.

It is stated that China is one of the world's oldest

civilizations, but it has become a recognized modern nation. The country has an estimated population of 1.4 billion. China at this time has more established citizens than all other countries. Most of the population live in the cities, while a large number of the people live in the country territories.

China's Kongfuzi, known to many as Confucius, taught people the value of such things as kindness, education, and a search into one's morality.

The dragon is seen and regarded as a symbol of good fortune to the people. Chinese emperors called themselves dragons, as well as their sons. This was due to the belief that they were born with the power to rule the country. The antithesis of the dragon is the phoenix, representing feminine power. Both creatures are auspicious in Chinese culture.

Many have heard of the painful practice of foot-binding, which entailed curling young girls' feet to modify their shape. Foot-binding began during what was called the "Northern Song period" between 960 to 1127.

The Yiren

The Yiren, a cryptid, bipedal hominid creature, has

been compared to the North American Sasquatch, also known as Bigfoot, and is said to dwell in the heavily forested regions of Hubei territory. The Yiren is also referred to by some as the monkey man, the Chinese wildman, or the Yeren. Records show the first documented sighting to take place was by a biologist named Wang Zelin.

Some believe it could be an orangutan that has evolved to bipedalism. Thus giving an appearance of a Bigfoot/Sasquatch. Could it be the missing link? Some believe it could be so. Bipedalism has evolved in the ape family a minimum of twice. There is speculation that this has happened again within orangutans.

The beast has been described by eyewitnesses as having thick reddish fur, but also some have stated the fur to be white. Standing in the seven-to-eight-foot-height range, the Yiren's appearance is said to be similar to that of *Gigantopithecus*, an extinct primate. Some believe that the Yiren is an ancient great ape surviving on the edge of civilization. Others speculate that the Yiren is a new species of orangutan or a misidentified monkey.

It is said that there have been well over four hundred Yiren sightings in the last century, according to a couple of news agencies. With that said, there are stories of this creature dating back to fourth-century China.

Today, the Yiren is said to have become a popular attraction to tourists and explorers. Every year, hundreds of people travel to the area of Shennongjia in hopes to set their eyes on the fabled Yiren. In the province's national park, there is a statue erected of the creature for visitors to the area to take a picture with.

Sky Serpents

Sky Serpents, also known to many as Sky Snakes, or even Sky Worms, are described as resembling long snakelike serpentine creatures. They are observed and documented as slithering through the sky. Some believe the serpent could be a dragon, but there is a notable difference between a Sky Serpent and a dragon in appearance. So they are not believed to be of the same family. The only similarity the sky serpents shares with the dragon comes from eyewitnesses who have claimed they can breathe fire. Some have described the flame to resemble lightning.

Many believe they are supernatural and not of flesh and blood. It's said by some that they can show up and disappear without warning. As a spirit can manifest itself, there is speculation that the Sky Serpent also may have the same ability.

Portals are another way it is believed the serpents are able to appear and then vanish. Many, when they think of a portal type door allowing one to jump from dimension to dimension, associate them to only exist in forests and houses that are perceived to be haunted or inhabited by a spirit or spirits. But with much research and conversations with both believers and skeptics, all believe a portal can exist in any type of natural setting.

Another theory falls under the subject of ufology. Some believe the creature could be of an extraterrestrial origin, seen flying and diving in the sky at the same time there have been reports of some type of alien or out-of-this-world spacecraft had been spotted. The ability to appear and disappear under this theory is associated with such beliefs of them being able to be "beamed up or beamed out of the spacecraft." Or the spacecraft has the ability to become "invisible" to the naked eye, at which some say the creature appearing and disappearing is the result of the being exiting the craft and re-entering.

There has been speculation that the Sky Serpents have been seen in other countries, but the belief is the first such reports originated in China.

The Guai Wu

The Guai Wu, a serpentine seal, lake creature, was first witnessed in the year 1903. It's believed that there are more than one, and they are said to dwell and can be found in the hard-to-reach volcanic Tianchi Lake, also known as Heaven Lake, in the northern province of Jilin. Sources claim the creature came from a volcanic eruption that should have obliviated any life in the lake, but instead opened up, from underground, a pathway for these creatures to escape into the lake. There have been over four hundred sightings to date.

Descriptions of the creatures by eyewitnesses claim them having a long, thick, gray to black body, flippers on each side of its serpentine torso, with a head that resembles that of a seal. Others have claimed the creature to have a head that very closely resembles that of a plesiosaurus. This description of the creature somewhat resembles Nessie, the Loch Ness Monster, of Scotland. Some witnesses have voiced that it even has a human-like face.

Eyewitnesses have claimed that the creatures have been seen fighting, or what some believe to be mating, in the lake. In the earlier 1900s, there were a few claims of attacks, but nothing since then. Some of the encounters, or attacks, were said to have been while folks were swimming, bathing, and with men fishing in boats. The creature was said to have flipped the watercraft over, spilling the men into the lake.

In 2007, there was a news reporter who captured what is believed to be six of the creatures swimming together in a photo. Two by two. It was reported that the speed of the creatures could be compared to that of a motorized boat. There is speculation of a video that was also taken at the time of the photo, but the video in question either doesn't exist or has been lost.

⬡

The Jinmenju

I haven't found much information on the Jinmenju, but it is said to be found in the southern territory of China. It's also referred to as the "human tree." It is said to grow smiling human heads as fruit. The seeds inside the fruit are also said to resemble a smiling face.

It's believed that when the fruit ripens, it is now able to be picked and eaten. The taste has been described as a little sour, yet also sweet to the taste. Many claim that you can hear the tree and its fruit laughing from miles away. Once in front of the tree, the laughter stops, and there is nothing but smiles staring at you.

4

Australia

Australia is positioned in the southern hemisphere and is surrounded by the Indian and Pacific Oceans. It is considered to be one of the driest and smallest of the seven continents. It is estimated that the Aboriginal people of Australia arrived in the territory over fifty thousand years ago from Asia by way of boat. Some also speak of them using a land bridge. They eventually divided into groups of families. Australia is one of the world's most ethnically diverse nations. Nearly a quarter of the people who live in Australia were born in other countries.

Australia is the only country in the world that covers an entire continent. It is one of the largest countries on the planet. Many Australian cities and farms are located in the southwest and southeast, where the climate is considered to be more comfortable to reside in. The territories vary in scenery, such as the northeast has dense rain forests, while southern territories have large deserts, with very little vegetation.

Gold was discovered in Australia in 1851. This discovery set in motion a rush to find riches, resulting in thousands of new immigrants. In the year 1859, six separate colonies were formed. In the year 1901, these colonies joined and formed what is called the British Commonwealth. The British Commonwealth covers all territories.

Australia is home to many of the deadliest species on the planet. There are over twenty types of venomous snakes and thirty-six species of poisonous funnel-web spiders in the eastern territory of Australia.

The Yara-ma-yha-who

The Yara-ma-yha-who came from Aboriginal legend and folklore. The creature is referred to as and has been given the nickname "the Australian Vampire." Described by some as resembling a reptilian demon creature. The creature is also said to resemble a frog or even a goblin-type creature. Said to be short in stature, around four feet tall, with red skin, and in some cases having long straggly red hair on its head, reaching down to the middle of its back. He has no teeth and is said to feast on humans, sucking the blood from their bodies.

The Yara-ma-yha-who is said to hide away in fig trees in a hunt for any victim to pass beneath. Once an unsuspecting individual attempts to pass under the branches, the creature will then jump upon the human and attempt to suck the victim's blood out through octopus-type suction cups located on the creature's hands and feet.

The Yara-ma-yha-who can also unhinge its jaw like that of a snake. Once the creature is finished devouring the body of the unlucky victim, it's said it will then regurgitate the body and take a nap. It is said that if the Yara-ma-yha-who awakens from his nap and devours the body again, multiple times, the human will once again come to life, but it will become a Yara-ma-yha-who as well.

It is said that Yara-ma-yha-who attacks can be avoided. If one is to play dead and not fight back once attacked, the creature will then move on. They are only interested in the living. Should one look for shelter under a fig tree for the night, they should slowly crawl up to where the tree exits the ground, and stay completely still and motionless until nightfall. It's said once the sun sets and the dark of night swallows up the territory, the Yara-ma-yha-who will be unable to leave the tree to attack.

———

The Hawkesbury River Monster

The Hawkesbury River Monster, also known as Moolyewonk or Mirreeular, is found in the Hawkesbury River in New South Wales, Australia. It is an extremely deep river, so it can certainly house a large serpentine creature. Described as an aquatic serpentine lizard and often compared to Nessie, the Loch Ness Monster of Scotland, many believe the creature to be a prehistoric plesiosaur. The plesiosaur is said to have been extinct for over seventy million years.

Eyewitnesses describe the creature as having two sets of flippers and a long, thin snakelike neck and slender round head. Some believe the creature to be anywhere from fifty to seventy feet long, with grayish-colored skin. Some have described the skin as smooth looking, while others have claimed the creature has a rough scaly-looking body. It's believed that the differ-ence in the skin texture could be the creature possibly shedding its skin, making it look rough, and possibly having scales.

It is believed the indigenous Dharuk tribe were the first to encounter and speak of the river monster. There has been a discovery of Aboriginal rock art, which is believed to date back well over four thousand years, in the area that describes what we now call the Hawkesbury River Monster. There have been multiple sightings year after year and recent eyewitness accounts. While some might believe that the creature is just a myth, with the recent encounters, it should be considered as so much more.

There are countless stories that have been passed down of men, women, and children being attacked. Many of the stories are those of boats that have been found overturned, with no sign of their occupants. Some boats have even been found along the shore, beat up, and some say with deep dig marks on the craft that most believe to be teeth marks from the creature. Swimmers, and even those who chose to bathe close to the shore area, have gone missing.

Bunyip

Bunyip, a spirit monster from Australian Aborigine culture. Bunyip translates in Aboriginal to mean evil or devil spirit, but is also known as Kianpraty. Bunyip in the Wemba-Wemba language means "devil." It's believed to dwell and sleep in rivers, swamps, water-holes, and billabongs during the day, but is said to lurk the land by night, looking for animals and humans to devour. It is believed that children and livestock are the creature's favorite prey. It is said it has a vocal scream that is so intense and loud, it can be heard for miles. The Aboriginals used to tell tales of many serpentine creatures that are believed to dwell in the waters.

The Australian residents have had many sightings and encounters over the years with the creature. Eyewitness accounts have described the creature as having dark fur, with a doglike snout upon the face. Others have claimed the beast resembles a snake man, with a long thick beard and tusks like a seal. While others describe a creature resembling both an alligator and a tall emu-like bird, with a long bill, the body most resembling that of an alligator. The hind legs are said to be extremely strong and muscular, and the front legs to be long and somewhat thin. The aquatic mammal is said to have long sharp claws on the tips of its toes, which are used to tear apart its prey, which in most cases are humans who happen to cross paths with the beast.

When it exits the water and goes on solid ground, it is believed to walk on its hind legs bipedally. Eyewitnesses believe the creature to stand as tall as twelve feet in height. When on land, it can run at a high rate of speed. In most cases, nothing can escape once it has set its eyes upon what it sees to be its next meal.

———

Muldjewangk

Muldjewangk are dragon-like creatures that inhabit the Murray River and Lake Alexandrina, which flows in South Australia. A hideous creature is said to lurk beneath the surface of the muddy waters. The tales of the aquatic creature were first told in an attempt to keep children away from the waters, which could be dangerous. The children were told to be very careful where they step, and to stay clear of any clumps of seaweed they see floating on the surface of the water. It is believed the Muldjewangk uses these to cover and camouflage itself so humans will come close enough for them to attack and devour.

By some they are seen as a possible merman-like creature (a male version of a mermaid) that is half fish, and half man. It is believed that there are many that inhabit the lake and river, and they reproduce by mating with other aquatic life a couple of times a year.

The most told encounter with a Muldjewangk tells

of a European steamboat captain who shot a Muldjew-angk. Due to shooting the creature, it was said the captain became extremely ill, developing a lingering death from painful, excruciating red leaking blisters that covered the captain's entire body. The Muldjew-angk is blamed for many disappearances in the area, as well as many boat wrecks. Many fishermen have discovered their nets destroyed at the hands of a Muld-jewangk.

The Yowie

The Yowie, the Australian hominid cryptid version of the North American Bigfoot, Sasquatch, or the Himalayan Yeti. The first known recorded encounter with the Yowie dates back to as early as 1876. It is believed they have been part of Aboriginal folklore and legend since much earlier than 1876. It is described as a large bipedal gorilla that is believed to live in the forested wilderness areas of Australia.

There is a theory that the Yowie also descends from the ancient and massive *Gigantopithecus*. There is another theory that they might be a living remnant of *Homo erectus*. Some theorize the Yowie could in fact be a bipedal marsupial, maybe descending from the extinct *Hulitherium*, which is in relation to the giant panda bear.

They are said to stand up to six or seven feet tall, with their bodies covered in black or brown hair. Although they are bipedal creatures, they have been reported as seen running on all fours. These hairy humanoids are said to be very humanlike in nature, displaying an intelligence not witnessed in other species. Most Yowie sightings are of solitary ones, but pairs and families have also been reported.

While most Sasquatch are considered to be "friendly," the Yowie is considered to be extremely aggressive and dangerous. It is said to have large talon-like claws. There have also been reports of the creature having two fang-like teeth that resemble a canine's jawline.

Many bizarre structures made of large sticks and branches, resembling man-made structures, are believed to be the work of a Yowie or a family of Yowies. Yowies are said to stay within the tree lines and try to hide behind bushes and thick vegetation in an attempt to remain unseen.

One encounter from 1997 was when a woman was awoken in the early hours of the morning by what she described as a large creature standing up to eight feet tall, covered in hair, and producing a horrible smell. It is said the encounter was investigated, and there was a discovery of large, nonhuman footprints in the area.

Many disappearances are believed to be the work of the Yowie. Some believe the creature will enter a residential area and attempt to kidnap women and children. Some believe the Yowie has even attempted to mate with an abducted woman. The creature is also suspect when it comes to missing pets. It is believed they kill, and eat chickens, pigs, and other livestock. Many have been seen eating fruits and rummaging through trash containers.

The Gippsland Phantom Cat

The Gippsland Phantom Cat is a large cat commonly known as the Blue Mountains panther and spotted in the Grampians region. The cat is considered by many to be a cryptid, and is studied by many cryptozoologists. The legend of the Phantom Cat is closely related to similar tales of unusual exotic felines or large cats that have been witnessed and reported for decades in the Blue Mountains territory.

There's a theory of how the cats may have come to be. Some believe that the origin of the Gippsland Phantom Cat can be traced back to animals let loose by United States soldiers based in Victoria, Australia, during World War II. A pair of pumas, or some type of other large cat, were said to have been used as mascots. Towards the end of the war, it was believed by many, the pumas were released in the Gippsland region.

This theory has yet to be proven, but with the reports of mass slaughter of livestock, it is considered by many as evidence to support the big cat theory. Reports state the livestock to be killed by a clean puncture wound, or long slit in the throat. The prey will then have its insides cleanly devoured. This type of kill and method of eating is in the same way a big cat kills and eats its prey.

The Carkit

The Carkit is a powerful spirit being that has been nicknamed the Australian Grim Reaper. It has been said by many explorers, squatters, and drovers for well over two hundred years that the Carkit will suddenly appear at one's campfire. The reaper will then abduct and take away one who is by the fire. It is believed the Carkit chooses who they will take based upon a bucket he carries full of names. If the bucket has one's name within it, that individual will be taken by the reaper, never to be seen again.

The Carkit will appear without warning and will speak the words, "It's time to kick the bucket." It is advised to "never" kick the bucket the reaper holds. It is said if the Carkit comes knocking at your doorstep, it would be best to ignore the visitor; do not let him in. If you do come face-to-face with the Carkit, make sure you fight with all your might. The people who do not fight back, and give up and give in, always in the end "kick the bucket."

5

South Africa

Twenty-four thousand years ago, tribes of hunters known as the San, or Bushmen, began moving into the territory. Many Sans to this day still live very much as their ancestors had, in the vicinity of the Kalahari Desert. Africa's landscape is made up of high, flat areas called plateaus. These lands are covered with rolling grasslands, called highveld, and tree-dotted plains called bushveld. Around the 1400s, European ships would dock on the South African coast to obtain much-needed supplies.

In 1963, Nelson Mandela, head of the anti-apartheid African National Congress, was sentenced to life in prison for what was considered "terrorist" activities. In 1990, after serving twenty-seven years of the sentence, he was freed by President F. W. De Klerk. In the year 1994, Mandela was elected president of South Africa, and he served in that position until 1999.

South Africa became a democratic republic after holding its first election on April 27, 1994. Many different backgrounds of people make up Africa's population; each have a history and language of their own. Due to this, the country has eleven languages. This colorful mix of cultures is how South Africa received its nickname the "rainbow nation."

To the south, east, and west territories of the plateau lands, you'll find a mountainous region referred to as the Great Escarpment. The eastern range is called the Drakensberg, but is also referred to as the Dragon's Mountain. The area has high peaks, some more than eleven thousand feet in height. In northern South Africa near the territory of Johannesburg, you'll find a cave formation referred to as the Sterkfontein. Archaeologists have uncovered human fossils. Some are believed to be more than two million years old. Due to this discovery, the region was given the nickname the "Cradle of Humankind."

As of the year 2022, the population in South Africa has hit 1,439,323,942.

Grootslang

Grootslang, the word means "great snake." The Grootslang is said to live within a cave referred to as the Wonder Hole, in the Richtersveld area of South Africa. The cave is said to have thousands of diamonds within it, but at this time no one can confirm the claim, for the Grootslang guards the entrance, tearing apart and devouring all who approach. The Grootslang is said to be part elephant and part serpentine and snakelike. The head is the part that resembles the elephant, with large elephant-like ears and tusks. The tail and the rest of the body are serpentlike. The monster is believed to be able to grow up to sixty feet long, with the body as thick as a whisky barrel.

One of the most intriguing aspects of this cryptid is the story of its creation. The tale is that of an amateur god who on their own was attempting to create a powerful creature. It is not confirmed what the reasoning was behind this, but some speculate it was a possible attempt to use this creature to overpower all other gods and become the most powerful of all gods. Being an amateur, the god made an unthinkable mistake, making this creature much too powerful. In order to stop the creature from having such powers, the elder gods decided to split the beast into two separate not-so-powerful animals, which is why the creature now resembles an elephant and a snake.

Legend tells that the Grootslang somehow escaped the overshadowing of the gods and was able to get away. This proved to be a larger issue than expected. When the gods caught up with the creature, it was discovered that the cryptid had been able to find a way to procreate and reproduce by mating with elephants.

The creature is said to also attack and eat anyone who comes near. It is said that there's a way to escape the wrath of the Grootslang if one were to come in contact. The Grootslang has a weakness for such items as diamonds and gems. It is taught that if you come in contact with the Grootslang, make sure you offer up any diamonds or gems you might have upon yourself as a trade for your life.

Some believe that the creature is just a large snake that has yet to be discovered and recognized by science. While others suggest the creature is some kind of prehistoric crocodile or alligator that has survived and awaits its next chance to ambush and devour its next victim.

The Inkanyamba

The Inkanyamba is a large carnivorous eel-like serpentine animal in the legends originating from the Xhosa and Zulu tribespeople of South Africa. These creatures are said to have long necks, horse or antelope-like heads, and a bulging spine running along their backs. They also have either large flippers or a pair of wings. It is said they can grow to tremendous sizes. The legend tells a tale of the Inkanyambas being able to somehow control the weather. There are actually fresh-water eels abundant in South Africa that grow to around six feet long, but that pales in comparison to the stories of the Inkanyamba.

The majority of sightings are said to take place at Howick Falls, which is on the Umgeni River in South Africa. Some zoologists believe or theorize it is a type of eel rather than a snake because it lives in lakes and waterfalls. Many believe it to be a large species of fresh-water eel, compared to that of the *Anguilla mossambica* or the *Anguilla marmorata*. Both of these eels can grow to about six feet in length.

According to the local natives of the area, the Inkanyamba have been witnessed and are said to be larger than a bear and have supernatural abilities. Sightings of this animal go way back to cave paintings that have been found on walls of caves inhabited by aboriginals, in the KwaZulu-Natal area. These paintings depict creatures that archaeologists have come to refer to as "rain animals" due to their association with vicious summer storms and being able to control the weather.

⸻

Kongamato

Described as a folkloric flying reptilian monster in Congo, Zambia, and Angola. It has been described by eyewitnesses as reddish in color, resembling a lizard with wings, and long, jagged sharp teeth protruding from its beak. The wingspan ranges from four to eight feet across. Those who believe in the Kongamato's existence claim the creature is a pterosaur, a prehistoric flying reptile from the dinosaur age. They theorize the creature survived in the swamps of Africa and had successfully hidden itself. The tribespeople also refer to the Kongamato as a flying evil spirit or demon.

The beast has been reported to dive into rivers and lakes to overturn boats and drown people. This is how the creature got its name "over turner" or "breaker of boats" and "overwhelmed boats." The Kongamatos are believed to be responsible for many unexplained capsized canoes of the native people, as well as attacks on those who came close to the nearby waters. There are several historic reports of encounters with explorers being savagely attacked by what they described as a large, winged creature. Many have reported they received wounds from what they believe to be a Kongamato attack. The Kaonde people of Zambia would carry good luck charms known as "Muchi Wa Kongamato" when crossing any rivers or bodies of water. They believed the charm would protect them and their loved ones from any and all Kongamato attacks.

It is believed its diet consists of mostly fish, but also of humans. The Kongamato is also believed to dig up grave sites to steal and consume the remains of a human corpse. In Africa, the burial sites are said to be shallow and not deep so the creature can smell the decay.

The Popobawa

The Popobawa is a fairly recent creature reported in Tanzania and Zanzibar. The name Popobawa in Swahili translates to "bat wing." The creature is an evil spirit or demon. Considered to be a shapeshifter due to its ability to appear as a human during the day, but transforms into a one-eyed, bat-winged terror at night. It is also said the creature has a pungent odor that has been described as that of a rotting carcass.

Many reports of attacks come every couple of years, with a large number of reports in 1995. The Popobawa is said to visit homes by night and attacks men, women, and even children before passing on to another house in the area. These vicious nighttime attacks consist of both physical and sexual assaults. The Popobawa is said to sodomize both men and women. Those who survive such an attack are urged to tell others that they have been assaulted. It is believed if one who survives the attack doesn't tell others of the power of the creature, it will return repeatedly for visits. It is also said that those who refuse to believe in the creature will be visited by one at some point, and the attack will be so vicious, the body of the human will be unrecognizable.

Many who believe in the Popobawa will try to guard against an attack by spending the nights awake and outside of their homes. The family members are said to huddle around an open fire, with other families joining them. They will take turns standing guard and watching out for the creature.

For some, the Popobawa is believed as just a myth, with a rational explanation of what folks might actually be experiencing. The attacks via the Popobawa could in fact be what some recognize as "night terrors." Night terrors are believed to occur when one experiences hallucinations. It is believed this takes place somewhere in between lucidity and deep sleep. In the end, there is something that is very real happening, and the legend of the Popobawa should be taken seriously, and the warnings not be ignored.

Bili Ape

There are legends of mysterious unknown ape species in Africa. Many of these cryptids are described as something between a chimpanzee and a gorilla. In other territories the Bili Ape is known as the Bondo Mystery Ape. The name was given in 2003. Many believe the Bili Ape to be an unknown species that has now been discovered. Researchers believe it to be a large chimpanzee species, but they are said to behave more like gorillas.

Bili Apes are a highly aggressive giant ape. The ape is said to have a very flat face and a wide jawbone. They also have an overhanging brow ridge. They have narrow shoulders, but very muscular arms. As they age, they turn gray like most, but the gray develops very early in their life. The Bili Ape is believed to grow up to six feet tall and has been reported to walk bipedally at times. Most encounters, however, report the ape to be a knuckle-walker like most chimpanzees. Their footprints, which range from eleven to fourteen inches, are longer than the largest most common chimp and/or gorilla footprints recorded.

Sources claimed Bili Apes build nests like gorillas. Some reports describe the ape to howl or scream a loud vocal at the moon. It is also believed the Bili Apes would feast upon lions and leopards.

The J'ba FoFi

The J'ba FoFi, also known as the Congolese giant spider, lives deep in the Congo. The adult J'ba FoFi are said to resemble a giant tarantula, dark brown in color, and with a body measuring over thirty inches in circumference. When standing up in full stance, they are said to be as tall as a human, with a leg span of up to six feet. The giant spider has long prominent fangs and has an extremely potent venom. The eggs of the creature are said to be pale yellow or white in color and a peanut shape form. Hatchlings are said to be bright yellow in color, with a purple stomach.

The local natives of the area talk of the large webs spanning from tree to tree. The vegetation or leaves are used as a cover or camouflage, and they are known to cross over walking and game trails. In other areas of the territory, the giant spiders use a different web-spinning style. They are known to dig deep burrows under tree roots and cover the burrow with webs, which they camouflage with vegetation.

The people of the Congo speak of the giant Congolese entering their villages, killing livestock, and even killing small animals. Sadly, the spider is to blame for the deaths of some children. Some villagers claim to have seen one of the spiders snatch a dog, inject it with venom, then scurry back into the jungle still holding the dog. They are also said to prey upon monkeys. Many have witnessed such a gruesome attack.

The residents, when building their homes, build the huts with a steep-pitched thatched roof. The walls are tightly spaced and tightly mounted to the ground to help prevent spiders from being able to enter the inside.

An extremely popular encounter with a J'ba FoFi sighting took place in 1938, in the area of the Belgian Congo. This territory is now the Democratic Republic of the Congo. Reginald and Margurite Lloyd were driving on a jungle path when a large figure made its way out into the road just ahead of them. It was first believed to be a monkey or a small human being. As they came closer, they realized it was an enormous spider. They stopped the car to let the figure pass, but they couldn't believe what they were seeing.

One of the oldest reported sightings of the J'ba FoFi was in the 1890s. It was by an English missionary by the name of Arthur Simes. It is believed he was traveling and en route to a village in Uganda. It is reported that he came across a huge web that spread across the road. Some of the men who were with him became entangled in it. Simes began helping the men by cutting away the web. Suddenly, two large spiders with a leg span of around five feet appeared and viciously attacked the trapped men. Simes fired his pistol at the spiders and they ran off. Simes was able to release the men from the grips of the web, but it was too late. The men had been bitten by the large spiders. Shortly after the attack, the men died.

6

Germany

Germany, named the "Land of Poets, and Thinkers," first recorded humans settling in northern Europe over ten thousand years ago. It is believed to have taken place after the end of the last ice age. The first people to speak a language similar to modern German is said to have lived in the territory about five thousand years ago. It was still thousands of years before what we call Germany became a reality.

Early Germany was a combination of small states ruled by many kings. In the year 1871, the country was united, via alliances, by a politician by the name of Otto von Bismarck.

In the late nineteenth century, Germany began going head-to-head with other European countries in an attempt to set up colonies in both Africa and Asia.

These tensions led to World War I in 1914, the worst conflict the world had ever seen. Germany and its allies were defeated by France, Britain, the Soviet Union, and the United States.

Unfortunately, Adolf Hitler and the Nazi Party came to power in the year 1933. In 1939, Hitler invaded Poland, which was the start of World War II. During the war, Hitler created camps in Germany where sadly millions of Jewish people and others were murdered. The war ended in 1945, with the great news of the Germans' defeat, and Hitler committing suicide.

After World War II, Germany was divided into east and west. The country became the center of a standoff between the Soviet Union and other Western powers. This head-to-head confrontation lasted forty-four years and was named the Cold War. After losing World War II, Germany was in complete ruins. The western territory of Germany recovered, but the east territory, under communist control, fell far behind. After reunification in the year 1989, Germany spent billions of dollars to modernize the east.

Drude

Drude, a folklore creature originating from central Europe and also part of German mythology. To this day, it is still unclear where the original origin of the legend of these witches came from, with not much information about all of this legend.

It is said to attack individuals as they sleep. It is believed the Drude will invade one's dream to turn the dream into a hideous nightmare. It is described as a nocturnal, malevolent dream spirit or dream witch.

Descriptions very, but most describe an elf, hag-like being, or a kobold that can haunt individuals as they slumber. The Drude is believed to belong to a specific form of demons. It is said to have originated from Alfonso de Spina's hierarchy. The word "Drude" is also said to be used as a term for witch or spirit witch.

A vampiric witch that is well versed in the arts of black magic, it is believed that all the Drudes are women. It has the ability to shape-shift into an owl or bird at night, and is said to seek out only men; as legend tells, they are powerless against her.

She can be warded off with a Drude's Stone (Drudenstein), which is said to have a naturally occurring hole in the center of it. Another method is with a Drudenkreuz, which is a Drude's type of cross. The Drude Cross is believed to essentially be a pentagram.

Nachzehrer

Nachzehrer is described as an undead creature found in Poland and the northern territory of Germany. It has been described as a vampire, or even some kind of unexplainable ghoul by some. It is said the Nachzehrers will not suck the blood of the living, unlike those of most vampire theories. The creature is said to consume dead bodies for their nutrition. Unlike most vampire theories, it is believed they are not created by being bitten by another Nachzehrer, but are believed to rise from the dead after a recent human burial.

Legend also states that a dead human body in some cases will transform into a Nachzehrer when an accidental death or an unnatural death occurs. They can even kill you by ringing a church bell, which is said to bring death to all who hear. If one is to come in contact with a shadow of a Nachzehrer, it could result in death.

As the Nachzehrer is ghoul-like, they are not easily killed. Like the theory of the wooden stake to the heart, this will not result in their death. You will need to chop off their head. It is said that one would need to insert a coin in the mouth of the creature. The coin will then paralyze the Nachzehrer. Then make the final blow by chopping the head off its shoulders.

In order to accomplish this gruesome task, one would need to find a Nachzehrer that is asleep, and slip the coin into the mouth of the creature. You can find them lying in a grave, and you can strategically insert the coin. It is said that upon first glance of the creature in the grave, they will have one eye that appears to be open. One should only be concerned if both are open. When one eye is closed, the creature is in fact asleep and unaware that someone is hovering over them. It is believed many have accomplished this task, but those who have attempted and failed were never seen alive again. However, some of the unlucky individuals' corpses were discovered, mutilated, and in many cases parts of the body were missing and considered to have been eaten.

Krampus

The legend of Krampus dates back centuries, originating as a German Christmas tradition during the twelfth century. The legend of Krampus is an integral part of the celebrations surrounding the feast of Saint Nicholas. It is certainly a popular, yet terrifying mythological creature. Beginning in the early part of December, the children of Germany would start to hear of Krampus, or the Christmas devil. Krampus is described as a horned and devilish anthropomorphic goat creature, with a long tongue, fangs, and a set of pointed horns. He is extremely hairy, with either brown or black hair, and has cloven hooves.

Krampus in most cases is seen carrying chains for thrashing and swinging as a way of creating intimidation. He also is said to carry a whip or a large bundle of birch branches to spank any children who have been naughty. He also carries a sack strapped to his back to abduct the misbehaved children and drag them to a certain underworld, never to be seen again. Krampus is seen as an evil version of Santa Claus, but who also is said to punish parents who allow their children to misbehave.

Krampus doesn't just possess supernatural powers, but he also has demonic creatures that are known as his unholy elves. These creatures are to Krampus as the beloved elves in the north pole are to Santa Claus. As per German legend, it tells a tale that Krampus was a companion or helper to Saint Nicholas. It is obvious that this creature is the complete opposite to the character of Santa.

Krampus was believed to have been part of pagan

rituals associated with the celebration of the winter solstice. According to the Krampus legend, he is said to be the son of Hel. Hel is known as the Norse god of the underworld.

With Krampus becoming associated with Christmas, and the rapid spread of Christianity, the Catholic church banned him.

Krampus and St. Nicholas are said to arrive on the evening of December 5, which is referred to as "Krampus Night," or "Krampusnacht." While St. Nicholas goes on his way, rewarding the well-behaved children by leaving presents, Krampus, on the other hand, beats those who are naughty with branches. In some cases, many speak of him actually eating the mischievous and naughty. On the morning of December 6, well-behaved children will awaken to find well-deserved gifts, while others are said to awaken…maybe.

Still today in the twenty-first century, many countries continue to celebrate Krampusnacht with parades and festivals. The townsmen dress like demons and devils or as Krampus himself and flood the streets, pretending to chase after children and intimidating parents. More recently, the legend of Krampus has gained popularity in the United States. Krampus festivals are held across the country in such locations as New York City, Los Angeles, and Philadelphia.

―――

Alp

The Alps are an extremely unusual form of creatures and/or entity from German folklore. Another entity said to appear in one's dreams, turning the dream to a nightmare, in the middle of the night. The Alps are believed to be spirits or a demon. It is said they will appear during an individual's dream as they sleep. Not only are they said to possess and haunt one's dreams, they also are said to sit on the people's chests they are haunting. The weight and heaviness of the body causes one to wake up from the terror, sometimes causing paralysis and apnea. The victim awakes unable to move under the Alp's weight.

After these creatures appear in the dreams of men and women, it is said they will continue to haunt the individuals by creating nightmares of the person's most feared thoughts and phobias. An Alp is typically male, and its victims are usually female. An Alp attack is called an *Alpdruck*, or often *Alpdrücke*, which means "elf pressure."

They are grotesque and horrifying in appearance

and believed to be able to transform or shapeshift into butterflies, dogs, cats, pigs, or snakes. The Alp is often associated with vampires, as they like to drink blood. They are said to suck the blood through the breasts of humans. And this is the reason they prefer women, to get the extra taste of breast milk. Sexual attacks by the Alp are said to be rare, but do in fact happen. There are tales of women claiming while they are asleep, they have been awakened by some kind of entity having intercourse with them, which is believed to be an Alp attack.

Alps are also said to be very much mischievous and into pranks. Some pranks are said to be the ability to sour a family's milk, moving chairs as one goes to sit down, and even re-diapering a baby with an already changed and soiled diaper. If one wakes up and their hair is extra tangled, it is believed an Alp created what is called "elf knots." Legend states they will ride a family's horse to exhaustion during the nighttime hours, so it is so tired it cannot be used for any type of activity the following day.

Oddly, it is believed a child could become an Alp if a woman bites upon a horse's strap to ease their pain during childbirth. Also, a child born with hair on their palms may very well become an Alp. If a woman who is pregnant is attacked and bitten by a wild animal, the child may be born an Alp. Why? No one knows. Sadly, a stillborn infant can return from the grave and will haunt their family, especially the woman who carried the baby.

Tatzelwurm

Tatzelwurm is a cryptid type of dragon reported in several areas in Germany, Italy, Austria, and Switzerland. The cryptid goes by many regional names, such as Arassas, Praatzelwurm, Stollenwurm, Springwurm, and Bergstutzen.

Reports of this creature vary in description, from having a feline type face to an amphibian or serpentine reptile body, which is said to resemble a small Asian dragon. The most common description is of a snake- or lizard-like creature with a long tongue and sharp teeth, or fangs. The skin is covered in scales, with some areas having patches of hair. The creature has two front legs, or arms, but has no hind legs. The Tatzelwurm can grow up to six feet in length and can stand up on its long thick snakelike tail. Like many reptiles, the Tatzelwurm will produce a hissing noise when threatened.

The creature has an incredible enhanced ability to

balance and has super high sensory hearing and smell. The eyes are said to be shiny or bright in nature. The Tatzelwurm is also said to be venomous and has the capabilities to kill a human with just one bite. Unlike any reptilian, it has the ability to drain one of their blood. The creature is also believed to have acid in its blood. Due to this, the being is said to be able to produce poisonous fumes into the air, debilitating anyone or anything, allowing the beast to attack.

The Tatzelwurm is said to be extremely quick and agile in order to quickly subdue any prey or threat they encounter. It is easily able to hide in vegetation and attack or ambush without any warning. Some believe it has the uncanny ability to leap great distances, and it is often witnessed soaring through the air.

One of the most infamous experiences with the Tatzelwurm was with a photographer by the name of Balkin. While in the territory of Meiringen, Switzerland, Balkin attempted to photograph what he believed to be an unusual-looking thick log. Much to his surprise, as he went to take the shot, the log moved and slipped away. There was a photo that was presented, but there was much scrutiny, as many believed it to be fake.

Tatzelwurm sightings have continued to the present day, but it is believed by many that the Tatzelwurm is a rare salamander, or specifically a Gila monster. There are many similarities between the Tatzelwurm and the Gila monster. Both prefer to dwell and burrow underground, in mountainous areas. The Gila Monster is also said to be extremely venomous and one of the world's few or only venomous lizards.

7

Madagascar

Madagascar has only been inhabited by humans for about 1,300 years. The first to settle on the island are believed to have arrived from Southeast Asia, coming in from Indonesia. History tells us that many small kingdoms ruled different territories of the island. France invaded the island in the year 1883. After World War II, in 1947, locals fought for their independence in what was known as the Malagasy Uprising. In the year 1960, Madagascar became an independent nation. Madagascar is a semi-presidential republic.

The people of Madagascar elect a president who, once in office, will choose a prime minister to put together a cabinet to advise the president. Madagascar's constitution was established in the year 1992. The prime minister is in charge of the judicial branches and the legislation, and they are in charge of establishing the laws.

Most of the country's population lives on the eastern half of the island, but many folks also live in the central highland's territory, not far from Antananarivo, the capital city. Madagascar is said to have a very youthful population, consisting of just over 60 percent of its residents only in their mid to late twenties. Music has been an extremely important part of the people's culture. Villages will hold parties that will consist of music and dancing. The whole village will take part in the celebration.

The territory of Madagascar consists of deserts, grassy plains, and rainforests. Eighty percent of Madagascar's economy is fueled by agricultural industries, including fishing and forestry. Among the island's most frequently sold agricultural products are coffee, vanilla, and sugarcane.

Fangalobolo

The Fangalobolo is reported to dwell in the Ankarana Reserve in the Northern territory of Madagascar. It was actually featured in an episode of *Destination Truth*. The team was led by none other than archaeologist and explorer Joshua Gates.

It is described to be a large bat and can grow in size larger than a golden eagle and standing over four feet tall and having a wingspan of over six feet from tip to tip. Like most bats, it is said to be nocturnal. The head and face are very different from the average bat. Some say the face resembles that of a feline, but has large wide ears, and eyes black as night. The Fangalobolo at times has been described as humanlike, having thin pale lips. The arms that extend into the wings, like all bats, are said to be muscular, and even veins can be seen if one is close enough. Many claim the creature to not have legs or feet you would see on a normal bat, but it has long muscular legs, with long toes. On the end of the toes, you'll find long thick jagged nails or claws the Fangalobolo will use to hunt or attack.

The Fangalobolo is said to be the protector of all the smaller and more vulnerable species of bats. It is said the large bat will fly and make its way through the crevasses of a cave and will wrap its large wings around and protect and share warmth like a blanket with the smaller bats. The Fangalobolo also acts as a deterrent to all predators that could be a potential threat to the colony, such as birds, snakes, and even humans.

Many who have witnessed and have been attacked

by the bat were those who were out wandering at night or in caves. One unlucky individual who was visiting the area was into cave exploration, documenting different caverns and caves around the world. He was deep within a cave that was very narrow, and the ceiling of the cave at some points hung low. When he came to one area of the cave, he noticed the bat droppings. He also noticed droppings that seemed to be much larger than what he was used to coming across.

As he went to back out, so as not to disturb any population of bats within the area, he tripped, causing his flashlight to shine up at the ceiling. At that moment, what looked like a large figure with wings darted down at him. He used his backpack to fight off the creature. As he was trying to exit the cave, he was knocked to the ground by a powerful force. He crawled to the exit and out into the sunlight. He looked back, but there was nothing there. There have been many other recorded and frightening stories to explore about the Fangalobolo.

Kalanoro

The Kalanoro is said to be a humanoid-type cryptid, but also said to be of spirit, and living inside the territory of Madagascar. The Kalanoro are thought to be spirits of nature, but can manifest into flesh form. It is believed these creatures can be found all across the lands of Madagascar. Many Kalanoro encounters are said to be extremely rare, but many more individuals are coming forward with such an encounter. The Kalanoro has been accused of the abduction of children, for an unknown reason. It is believed that when the creature is in search of food within Madagascar's villages, eyewitnesses have claimed to have seen the creature grab a child and disappear.

Many tribes in other areas of the island certainly agree the Kalanoro does in fact exist, but the creature is known by many different names, such as Vazimba or Kotoky. The Tsimihety and Antakarana tribespeople believe the Kalanoro in their region mostly dwells in caverns and/or caves. It is said, according to the people who call Madagascar their home, that the Kalanoro has a history of dwelling and existing on the island for well over two thousand years. Reports go as far back to the people who first migrated to the island stating they had an encounter with this beast.

This humanoid cryptid is generally described as being anywhere from two to four feet tall. Resembling something like a small Sasquatch, but with troll-like features as well. The creature is also said to have hooklike fingers, with long narrow flesh-ripping fingernails, and is said to have three to four backward-facing toes. The arms are long with a thin, yet muscular appearance.

It is believed the Kalanoro possess dark magical powers. The Kalanoro's long hair is where the powers and the strength of the creatures' supernatural abilities are said to come from, or where they are stored. The powers of the being are believed to be transferable to some herbalists (Mosies) who reside in Madagascar. The claim is that any type of potions mixed of magical powders and mixed with Kalanoro hair will provide the users with unusual and great mystical powers. Madagascar Mosies are said to also act as mediums. The Mosies claim the spirit side of the Kalanoro holds great healing powers, able to cure many sicknesses, and be cured of any curse that may have come upon them.

Vegetables, grain, and even raw seafood are said to make up the diet of the Kalanoro being.

The Drekavac

The Drekavac, also referred to as the Screamer, Drekalo, Krekavac, or Zrikavac, is believed to be a materialized manifestation of a dead, unbaptized human being.

One interesting legend tells of a young boy who passed away unexpectedly in a horrific death due to another's negligent actions. Due to this, he cannot find peace in the afterworld, so he haunts anyone and everyone, and especially the one who destroyed and is responsible for him losing his life.

The description of a Drekavac via eyewitnesses speaks of a small, yet furry or hairy being that is similar to an aye-aye, which is a type of lemur endemic to Madagascar. There are individuals who have described the appearance to resemble very much that of a Chupacabra, which many believe to be a form of devil canine, while some believe it has extraterrestrial origins. The Drekavac is said to have an ungodly scream, which people say that they have heard on multiple occasions in the middle of the night. Some even claim at times the vocal can resemble a child crying and even the howling of wolves or wild canines. In some areas it is believed that those who hear a scream of the Drekavac are in fact are only a few days away from experiencing an untimely death. If the Drekavac appears in the form of a child, that would mean an immediate death of a person. In the territories of Croatia, Bosnia, and

Serbia, it is believed a vocal scream from the Drekavac is a harbinger of death.

The Drekavac can be found often in the dark shadows, wandering the graveyards and cemeteries at night. The creature is said to hate the light of day and is mostly nocturnal in nature. The being will attack and strangle sleeping individuals throughout the evening, not letting up until the body of the victim stops twitching. They will also hunt and attack humans who find themselves near the cemeteries or forests. They are said to jump on the backs of the humans and force them to walk all night until the dawn of day. Unless the victim complies with the demand of the Drekavac, the being will leave his victim mutilated. The demands are never the same, so there is no way to be prepared.

One aspect among many that makes this being terrifying is it can't be killed or destroyed. The only way to rid the creature from walking the earth is to help it find its peace. The most popular and express way of resolving the issue of the Drekavac is to somehow baptize the creature.

Giant Fossa

Cryptoprocta spelea is not a myth or legend and is also

known as the Giant Fossa, in the family Eupleridae, which is closely related to the mongooses and includes all Malagasy carnivorans. The Giant Fossa is an extinct species of carnivore from Madagascar. It was first scientifically represented in 1902, and in 1935 was recognized as a separate species from its closest relative, the living fossa. *C. spelea* was much larger than the fossa, but otherwise similar. The two have not always been accepted as a species. How and when *C. spelea* went extinct is unknown to this day.

With it not known when the Giant Fossa became extinct, there is some evidence, weak evidence, that there is more than one fossa still surviving today. There are two fossa species, and there are some similarities and differences between the two.

The giant fossa was large and had huge teeth and jaws. It was a hunter or a predator. It had been said to fit the description of a large feline such as a mountain lion, or puma. Some say lemurs were the main prey, but other such prey would include euplerids and tenrecs. It is believed with the extinction of the Giant Fossa, this may have changed the food chain and dynamics in Madagascar.

The Madagascar Man-Eating Tree

The Madagascar tree, also known as "YA-TV-EO," is allegedly a man-eating tree that resides on the African island of Madagascar. The legendary tree is a carnivorous plant said to be large enough to kill and consume a human or some type of large animal. A quick reference: many picture the plant from the hit movie *Little Shop of Horrors*.

The first, or earliest tale of a man-eating tree came via a report by Edmund Spencer. The article by Spencer was first printed and appeared in the daily edition of the *New York World* on April 26, 1874. It also was printed and appeared again in the weekly edition of the newspaper two to three days later. In the article, there was a letter published regarding a German explorer by the name of Karl Liche. Liche spoke of witnessing a gruesome sight, regarding a sacrifice carried out by a "native tribe," of Madagascar. This story was picked up by many other newspapers of the day, including the *South Australian Register* on October 27, 1874, where it gained even greater popularity.

The first tree Liche encountered, he described as having an eight-foot-tall trunk that was dark brown in color and shaped like a pear or a pineapple. Found near the top of the tree, he described eight leaves, each ranging from ten to twelve feet in length and up to five feet in width. The sides of the leaves that faced up to the sky were covered with sharp, black thorny-like hooks.

On the very top of the tree there was what can be described as an oval-shaped opening or cavity that held and was filled with some form of liquid. Some believe this liquid could be to the tree as acid in the stomach is to a human. It helps break down whatever it consumes. Six long, tall tentacles reach out from the base of the cavity opening. They are described as looking extremely snakelike, but also resembling a tarantula leg, with hair covering the extremity.

Chase Osborne, another explorer, corroborated Liche's account of the tree in 1914. Osborne at no time ever laid his eyes on the tree himself. His claim that the deadly tree did in fact exist came via testimony of local missionaries and of the local tribespeople who dwelled in the area. But they warned for all to stay clear and avoid the exploration and any study of the tree.

8

Haiti

Haiti shares the island with the Dominican Republic and has been inhabited since around 5,000 BC, when Explorer Christopher Columbus docked on the island of Hispaniola in 1492. He then claimed it to be a Spanish colony. Due to this, hundreds of Spanish settlers arrived and took over the territory. Haiti is one of the most congested and densely populated countries in the world. It is estimated that there are around one thousand people for every square mile. The majority of the population lives in rural territories as laborers, working as farmers. Haiti's capital is Port-au-Prince and is the most populated city, with nearly three million residents.

Haiti's government is a semi-presidential republic, with a president acting as the country's leader, and a prime minister reports directly to the president. The president is elected to office every five years by a majority vote by the people of Haiti. The president, once voted in, will appoint the country's prime minister.

One of the country's official languages is Haitian Creole, a mixture of French and African languages, which is spoken by the majority of the population. French is also an official language, but only about 10 percent of Haitians speak it. Many Haitians practice voodoo, which combines West African spiritualism with the worship of Roman Catholic saints. In 2003, voodoo was declared an official religion. Today, marriages and other ceremonies held in the voodoo tradition are recognized by the government.

Haiti's climate is tropical with warm temperatures present most of the year. While some of the territory in the country is mountainous, the coastline is flat and covered with coconut trees. Haiti is just a bit smaller than the US state of Maryland in comparison. It has many climate zones that are very diverse, including territories of dry forests. This is where one would find several different species of cacti grow, and the coastal mangrove forests where the American flamingos are said to spend their time. There is a variety of species that inhabit Haiti such as the

Haitian boa, the Haiti national bird, and the Hispan-
iolan trogon.

———

Haiit

The Haiit is said to be a type of cryptid described
as around three to four feet tall and extremely strong
and fast. Eyewitnesses describe the creature as having
black and orange fur or hair and a small tail protruding
from its backside. The hands have long fingers with
sharp clawlike nails, while the feet have just three toes,
which extend out and, like the fingers, have long sharp
claws or daggerlike nails. Some describe the creature as
a mini-Sasquatch, while others give witness to a small,
bulky, muscular hair-covered human.

Those who've had encounters claim the Haiit is
extremely aggressive in nature and known to become
violent when approached or stumbled upon. The individuals who have come across its path or have come
close enough have reported being screamed at with a
violent type of vocal while jumping in a crazed manner
and picking up and throwing random objects to show
their dominance.

One such encounter with the Haiit is said to have
turned deadly. While three tribesmen were hunting,

one of the men came upon what is said to be a Haiit that was asleep. The tribesman startled the creature, and the man attempted to run and retreat. The creature lunged and, using the claws on both their hands and feet, began to shred the man's skin from the bone. The other men just stood in shock, knowing there was nothing they could do. They then turned and ran to avoid the same fate as their friend.

It is said that the latest sighting of a Haiit was by a man who was floating along the banks near the shore. He was casting and putting out nets, as well as checking the nets already in the water, when he heard an ungodly howl or scream coming from the nearby thick wooded area. In fright, he quickly stopped what he was doing and began to look around in a chaotic panic.

Out of a nearby tree dropped a Haiit into the water. The creature furiously lunged at the man as it made its way through the water to the man's boat. The creature grabbed the side of the boat and attempted to capsize and flip the boat with the man in it. In fear, the man used a baton-type bat and struck the aggressor. The creature then let go of the boat and retreated into the woods. But not before grabbing some items out of the boat.

The man made his way to land, where he encountered some native tribesmen. He told them of the attack. They replied that they called them Haiit pirates. For they will attack you and then attempt to steal from you.

The Caribbean Crowing Snake

The Caribbean Crowing Snake is seen and believed by some to be not just of flesh and blood, but of spirit. It's said to dwell and occupy the forests of eastern Haiti and is also found in parts of Jamaican territory.

The snake is said to be nocturnal and four to six feet long, with an unusually thick body. Many have claimed it resembles a telephone pole in width. Its color is said to be of a maroon or ochre type while covered with dark red or black spots. In mostly all reports, the witness mentions the tail of the serpent to be in a feathered type of tuft. The Crowing Snake is said to have a red crest upon its head and doesn't slither like most snakes, but waddles and sways back and forth like a rooster. Another unusual characteristic of the snake is it has a distinctive, yet familiar vocal. Not the usual hiss, but it's said to crow as a rooster does. The snake has been witnessed devouring humans, livestock, and family pets. Many of the unexplained disappearances of the tribespeople are believed to have fallen victim to the bizarre snake.

One such attack is told of the snake making its way into a village in the late hours of the evening. While the tribespeople slept, it is believed the snake entered the village at the south end. It is said it made its way into one of the homes, where it came across a teenage boy asleep on the ground. The next morning, the boy was missing, and the tribespeople discovered large markings that were identified as belonging to a snake, in the soft ground outside the home. The length of the snake could not be determined, but the width in some sections, which all believed was the snake leaving with the boy consumed within it, looked to be over fourteen inches wide. The teenage boy was never found.

At the end of the day, the modern belief is the snake is just mere local folklore used to scare young children into not wandering off. However, many people of Haiti disagree and insist that the creature is in fact real, and if one is to look deep enough, they would discover recorded historical cases of Crowing Snakes being captured and even killed. In the year 1829, what was believed to be a partially decomposed body of a Crowing Snake was allegedly examined by a doctor in Jamaica.

The snake is said to still roam the territory, in both flesh and spirit.

Caribbean Monk Seal

The Caribbean monk seal, whose scientific name is *Monachus tropicalus*, is also known by many as the sea wolf. The seal is said and believed to have gone extinct around the late 1940s to early 1950s. One aspect of a cryptozoologist is we do not just focus on legends and possible monsters, but we search for proof of species that are said to have gone extinct, but possibly have not. These seals are believed to be the only sea lion in the Caribbean, off the Gulf of Mexico. There is some debate on the actual claim of extinction. The monk seal once dwelled in the territories of Hispaniola and the West Indies.

The monk seal is described as having an extended muzzled face, which was very unique and not like other seals. The monk was extremely large and could grow up to seven or eight feet in length and weigh anywhere from five hundred pounds up to seven hundred. Caribbean monk seals were grayish and brown in color, with the underside being lighter. An adult seal's skin color is said to be much darker than the younger ones.

One group had a greenish tint, believed to be due to algae growing on their pelage. The life span of a monk seal is estimated to be eighteen to twenty years.

The Caribbean monk seal, sadly, was hunted to its extinction. Hunters targeted the seal, as they were slow and easily taken for their blubber. Years would soon pass, turning into decades, with no new recorded sightings. Even with teams of investigators and well-planned-out and executed expeditions, the teams all failed in their attempt to find any surviving monk seals. It was officially declared extinct in the year 2008.

However, regardless of the official announcement of extinction, divers, fishermen, swimmers, and many other individuals in the Jamacia and Haiti territories have reported over the years to have witnessed on many occasions what they believe to be a monk seal in various areas.

Mermaids

The Caribbean territory has held a long history of sightings and tales of mermaids and mermen. Many historical accounts of encounters with mermaids or mermen took place in the deep seas of Hispaniola. The mermaid, also known to some as sirens, plays a large role in many Caribbean folkloric traditions. In the rivers of Haiti, there are what are described as mythical merfolk, and they live in the river territory and are known to the locals as river maidens or water queens.

Many see the legend of mermaids and their appearance as majestic and that of beauty and grace. Such as the Disney character Ariel from *The Little Mermaid*. This is a common misconception. Most recorded sightings tell of an aquatic woman who calls to lonely sailors to come close to her. Some even say they will sing and put one in a trance, during which they want nothing but to come close to the being. The unlucky individual is then grabbed and pulled under the waves to first be drowned, then devoured.

In 1493, traveler and explorer Christopher Columbus claimed to have witnessed multiple mermaids or mermen on many occasions while sailing near the shores of the Dominican Republic. Columbus describes seeing what he believed to be three mermaids gathered together within the water. He claimed that they surfaced out of the depths of the sea right in front of him and his crew members.

Many believe that Columbus did not see any type of aquatic human, but in fact what he was witnessing was a group of manatees. As a longtime explorer and sailor, he would know the difference and not misidentify such a common sea dweller as the manatee as an actual mermaid.

John Smith, an English explorer, also made claims to have witnessed a mermaid in these waters in 1614. Smith saw the creature as sheer beauty, and he couldn't look away. He described the hair as long and wavy. There are reports that state Smith had possibly fallen in love with the sea maiden.

It is reported that Blackbeard the pirate himself, along with his whole crew of shipmates, witnessed what was believed by all to be mermaids on multiple occasions while sailing the waters of the Caribbean. To Blackbeard and his crew, seeing such a creature was considered a bad omen, and they believed it would bring disaster. Blackbeard was so superstitious and had such a fear of mermaids that many claim he would direct the crew to steer clear of any area or territory where they were thought to exist.

Haiti Werewolf

The Caribbean island nation of Haiti speaks of extremely dark lore regarding spiritual evil, voodoo spells, and even real-life zombies walking the territory both by day and by night. The zombies are said to be individuals who passed, but had a curse placed upon them prior to death. Now they walk the lands, looking for helpless wanderers to devour. With a thirst for human blood, they lurk in the shadows, awaiting their next meal.

Haiti has multiple versions of monster lore that are considered to be much like those talked about in other areas of the globe. One such monster, if you will, would be the Haiti werewolf, which the people of the territory refer to as "Red Eyes," "the Je-Rouges," "the French Loup Garou," and "the Lougarou." The lore surrounding these creatures in Haiti legend speaks of these creatures as powerful shapeshifting evil spirits who can transform and twist their bodies into an animal form, or just some ungodly abomination. Others speak of a person who has been possessed, and their body becomes overtaken by a nefarious spirit.

Werewolves, in most cases, are thought to be all male, and it is believed once an individual has completed the transformation, becoming a bipedal wolf, they will set out and hunt into the night to feed upon flesh and blood. There have been many men who have been hunted down and lynched when they were suspected to be a werewolf.

The creature is said to target livestock, pets, and humans. It is believed that children are preyed upon due to their innocence and lack of strength when an attack occurs. Legend of the Je-Rouges has haunted the people of Haiti for generations. The lore of these creatures spans across many religions and socioeconomic borders, with belief in these creatures strong especially among the poor. Far from being seen as a mere legend, many Haitians truly believe that these creatures do in fact exist among them, and many speak of frightening encounters with the beasts. This belief is so strong among the people that unexplained and strange deaths are in most cases believed to be the work of a werewolf.

Still to this day, there are frightening sightings, encounters, and multiple unexplained disappearances and mutilations reported.

9

Ecuador

Ecuador is located in the western corner at the top of the South American continent. Ecuador is roughly the size of the US State of Colorado and is bordered by Peru and Colombia. Ecuador was part of the Inca Empire. When the Spanish arrived, they claimed the country as a Spanish colony. For over three hundred years, the Spanish controlled the territory. In 1822, Ecuador established its independence from Spain.

The high Andes Mountains are the backbone of the country. Cotopaxi in the Andes is said to be the highest active volcano on the globe. The Oriente is east of the Andes and is rich in oil. The never-ending search for oil has caused environmental devastation, primarily due to oil leaks and destruction of forests.

Well over 10 percent of the population is of

European descent. Over 25 percent of the population are indigenous or native cultures, while the remainder are of mixed ethnicity. Many of the native people are subsistence farmers and only grow enough food for their family.

Ecuador is said to be one of the most diverse countries on the globe. There are over 1,600 bird species and well over 25,000 known plant species. The Galápagos Islands, 596 miles west of the mainland of Ecuador, are part of the territory and are home to unique plants, reptiles, and birds. The Costa, or coastal plain region, is where many of the world's bananas are grown.

Ecuador has eighteen islands, which are home to the Galápagos tortoise, the Galápagos penguin, the blue-footed booby, and iguanas.

Ecuadorean Giant

There are many legends surrounding giants walking the earth at one time. Many, when it comes to stories surrounding giant humans, refer to the biblical story of David and Goliath. There was also Robert Wadlow, known as the "Alton Giant." Wadlow, stood eight feet, eleven inches tall. Another spoken of often is the wrestling superstar sensation Andre the Giant, who stood seven feet, five inches. Andre, sadly, passed in 1993.

There are countless tales of unusual and interesting discoveries in Ecuador. Most recent was what is being referred to as the "Lost City of Giants." This was uncovered by a group of explorers in the jungles of Ecuador. In 2013, a huge skull believed to be female was found in the Salaam territory. Researchers and explorers, after carefully studying and running aging tests, believe the skull was well over six hundred years old. With the discovery of the skull, the group then set their focus on a careful search for the rest of the skeleton, which was finally gathered approximately a month later. The skeleton measured seven feet and four inches tall.

Due to this discovery, many researchers and explorers have ventured out on a mission to uncover more skeletal remains. A large number of the skeletons have been found in different parts of Ecuador, and even some on the border of Peru. Researchers believe these remains date back to the early fourteen to fifteen hundreds. The vast number of the skeletons discovered and documented were all between seven and nine feet tall and were found in what looked to be burial grave sites. The burials were elaborate. Bodies were wrapped in leaves and buried in thick clay. This sealed the skeletons and protected against water intrusion, leaving the remains in fairly good condition.

The reconstruction of the skeletal fragments found in Ecuador was erected in 2004 and can be witnessed and visited in Mystery Park in Interlaken, Switzerland.

Tshenkutshen

The Tshenkutshen, a feline or arboreal crypto marsupial is also known by many other names such as the howler monkey tiger, rainbow tiger, jaguar rainbow, tsenku-tsenku-yawá tsenkutsen, and tsenkutsen-yawá. The creature is believed to be the most ferocious and dangerous of all jungle animals by the Shuar people.

The description of a Tshenkutshen is compared to that of a jaguar in size and in appearance, but believed to be a bit smaller, according to some accounts. The cat is said to be dark gray to black in color. The chest area just under the throat has an unusual pattern with multi-colored stripes consisting of yellow, red, and white. The shoulders are said to have an unusually placed hump. Other strange features include monkey-like flat-palmed hands, with long sharp claws.

The cat is said to be extremely aggressive in nature

and territorial, attacking any other creature or human that wanders into what they see as their land. The beast has the ability to jump or leap from tree to tree due to its powerful strong muscles in both the front and hind legs. Some say the creature never walks on land, but uses just the trees, which works as a form of camouflage while hunting, and protects from the elements. The trees it chooses to dwell within are said to be near rivers and other bodies of water. In most cases, when witnessed, they are alone, but do at times hunt in pairs.

Bakru

Bakru, referred to as a dwarf spirit due to its size, is also known as Bakroe. It is said to be a troll, gnome, or dwarf type of spirit originating from the Winti religion of Suriname. The Bakru is deemed as a Busi Winti, which means forest or fire god. The Bakru is said to be approximately the size of a toddler, but with an extremely large or oversized head. The eyes are described as being large, round, and with a red glow.

The Bakru are commonly witnessed in pairs and are said to be located and found living near old trees or old houses, where it dwells with its family. The spirit is commonly witnessed under bridges and underpasses.

There is also a spirit Bakru, which is believed to be created by Wisi men, who are known and feared as evil. The Bakru designed by these men are said to be made of half wood and half human flesh.

There are a few known legends revolving around the creation of how the Bakru came to be. One legend is that a Bakru is first a piece of wood that has been possessed and brought to life. This piece of wood has a certain spell placed upon it with the spirit of someone or something unknown to man, which could be demonic. Another legend revolves around paralyzed or deformed humans. The deformities are why the appearance is seen as dwarf or troll like. Strangely, it is believed the humans are possessed. The humans are robbed of their sanity and will to fight and are used as slaves or servants by the evil Wisi men to perform tasks that are seen to be undesirable. If the Bakru cannot follow through on the demands or orders given because the person has died, the Bakru will have no choice but to bring violent harm upon the Wisi man who gave the orders or assignment.

The Bakru are fearless and will attack humans and are even believed to have raped women. When it attacks, it is said it will use the wooden part of its body to inflict wounds and to protect itself from any type of sharp objects or weapons. It cannot feel pain due to this strategy. The Bakru cannot think for itself; its mind is in such a trancelike state, it will just focus on whatever task is put before it.

The Bakru are ordered to perform such evil tasks for the Wisi men that just the mention of the name Bakru strikes terror and fear in all who hear it. It is to only obey the words or demands of the Winti. Like with many legends, when it comes to unexplained murders, disappearances, and possession, the blame is easily put upon the Bakru.

The Chuzalongo

The legend of the Chuzalongo has long been a discussion of fear in the Ecuador territory. A mythological being of the Quichua tribespeople and the Mestizo people, the Chuzalongo is an evil entity who lives in the mountains and is said to leave small footprints that seem to just stop as if the one leaving them has vanished. Many have set out in an attempt to find and capture him, but no one has been successful in their attempts. The Chuzalongo is said to appear as a child to lure in any unsuspecting humans. Once close enough, he will then transform into a hideous monstrosity full of pure evil and can kill even with his gaze. There are versions of the legend regarding the Chuzalongo that tell tales of attacks on men when they are working alone harvesting in the field.

The legend speaks of a farmer and his two young daughters who fell victim to unspeakable evil. They lived and raised cattle on the top of a mountain. One evening, as an extremely strong storm hit the territory, the farmer became concerned about the cattle and their safety. So he sent his two daughters to retrieve the cattle and secure them in the barn. The two daughters headed out to complete the task ordered by their father. They gathered and led the livestock into the barn one by one. When they finished, they closed and secured the barn doors.

As they turned around to head back to the safety of their home, they were frightened by what appeared to be some small sort of human. The being stood there with an extremely pale, white face, an unusual flat nose, large thick purple lips, large wide ears, and unusually small green beady eyes. The pupil of each eye had what looked to be a black dot or spot. The hair of the creature, or being, was blond or light red in color and often falling out of the scalp and onto the ground. The body looked to be covered with fish scales or a rough brown texture of skin.

They screamed at the sight of the creature, but with

the noise from the storm winds, their father could not hear their cries for help.

After some time had passed, the father became concerned that his two daughters had not yet returned home. The father took his shotgun and ventured out of the home to find his daughters. As he approached the barn, he came across a horrible scene. His daughters had been dismembered. In the distance, he saw what looked to be a small creature running away. He shot at the being but, sadly, was not able to avenge his daughters' deaths.

Mapinguari

The Mapinguari or Mapinguary, which means roaring animal, is a cryptid reported in the Ecuador territory, among others. According to legend, thousands of years ago, the Mapinguari or Mapinguary was once believed to be an Amazonian shaman who discovered and took advantage of the key to immortality. This discovery and misuse of the power angered the gods. The gods acted and severely punished the shaman. The gods cast an irreversible curse upon the man, which transformed him into a bipedal, wild, hairy abomination. This wandering beast dwells and spends its time in the forests, lurking, and always in search of food. While some claim the creature to be a guardian and protector of the forests, other stories speak of a creature that aggressively tears down bushes and trees daily.

The appearance of the creature is said to be primate in nature, standing bipedal at over seven feet tall, much like the known Sasquatch, or Bigfoot creature. However, the beast has been witnessed running on all fours. Some claim the body to be covered with dark matted reddish fur, while others have claimed dark to black. The entire body is thick and muscular with long legs. This apelike creature is said to have a flat snout, with jagged teeth protruding from its jaw, with black eyes. There are some who have claimed the Mapinguari only has one eye, such as a cyclops.

Both the feet and fingers have jagged long claws. When startled, it is said to stand on its hind legs and attack. Not all accounts speak of an odor, but it has been recorded that there is an awful odor that exudes from the creature's matted and knotted fur. A few interesting characteristics are the beast is said to have a large opening or gap-like mouth in its stomach area. It is believed this is how the creature devours whatever it catches to feast upon. The feet are said to be backwards, but the creature can easily walk forward, but can run backwards at a high rate of speed. Also, there have been many claims to the beast being unable to be killed, and due to the thick matted fur, no bullets can penetrate and make it to the creature's flesh. Many cryptozoologists speculate that the Mapinguari is a medium-sized giant ground sloth from the Ice Age that once inhabited and lived in the area.

Another theory is the creature is a Curupira. This legend is an entity that is said to protect the forests and animals from poachers and hunters. Why many believe the Curupira to be one and the same as the Mapinguari is the fact both have feet that are said to be backwards and can run backwards. However, the Curupira is said to be much shorter in height than the Mapinguari.

According to the Curupira legend, the creature is a boy who wanders through the woods in an attempt to confuse and disorient hunters, lumberjacks, and anyone who plans to bring harm or damages their habitat. The Curupira is able to do this because it has the ability to leave people stunned with just a whistle. The person becomes extremely dizzy and develops a headache. This leaves the individual lost and wandering, while unable to find their way back home.

10

Ghana

There are well over fifty different ethnic groups in Ghana, each having their own languages and customs. The Akan people are the largest tribe and make up over 45 percent of the population. They live mostly in villages and harvest their food on farms. Children in Ghana begin attending school at age four, which is kindergarten and lasts two years. The children between ages six and twelve are expected to attend six years at an elementary school. Ghana's school system in many ways is far more advanced than many of the African school systems. The capital of Ghana is Accra, and with the country's love of soccer, there is a large stadium built in the area.

The president, like most countries, is the head of government in Ghana. The president and their vice president are elected to office every four years. There is also a system of tribal government in addition to the national government.

Ghana has national parks and many nature reserves. These locations are set up to help protect the wildlife in the Ghana territory. The Kakum National Park is home to such wildlife as flying squirrels, African gray parrots, leopards, and monkeys. Pythons are native to the territory, as are some venomous snakes such as the puff adder and cobra. Elephants, buffalo, antelope, and leopards are found in the area, but mostly in nature reserves due to a decline in the populations from hunting and poachers. In the Mole National Park territory, one will have an opportunity to witness elephants, crocodiles, and hippos. Most are witnessed by watering holes in the park.

Ghanaians are very skilled in their arts. They are said to eat gourd-like fruit that they then make into barrels from the trunk. They also utilize natural resources, such as the bark of a tree, to make such items as clothing, harnesses, and ropes.

Sasabonsam

A Sasabonsam, also known by other names such as

Asanbosam, Asasabonsam, Sammantam, Shamantin, is a type of vampire or flying humanoid from Ghana legend and folklore. The legend dates as far back as 1897. Sculptures have been molded based on the legend's history, which speaks of a bearded human face, a pair of pointed horns, which some believe could be ears, long hair with a thin emaciated body, short stub-like limbs, twisted legs, and wings that resemble those of a bat.

This large humanoid creature, according to witnesses who lived to tell the tale, has long sharp teeth that look to be made of iron, and long hooklike claws. The skin is said to be dark pink to almost red in color. Some, due to the appearance and skin color, believe the creature to be Satan himself or a servant of the underworld. Some have spoken of a feeling of dread once in the presence of or believed to be close to a Sasabonsam.

The Sasabonsam are said to live and dwell within the shadows of the treetops. Their hooklike claws are used to attack, capture, and tear apart their prey. Also believed to be cannibalistic in nature, their evil soul delights in the mutilation and overall suffering of both animals and humans once captured. Once the animal or unlucky wanderer is subdued, the blood will be drained and consumed. Their wings are said to be extremely long in length. Some legends tell a tale of fifteen to twenty feet in wingspan, while others claim a bit smaller at ten to fifteen feet. The wings protrude out of the sides of the creature's back and are thin with visible veins running from the bulk of the body to the tip of the wing.

As in many legends passed down over the years, here you'll find another creature who is believed to be suspect and responsible for multiple unexplained disappearances, unexplained deaths, and mutilations on livestock, pets, and humans. One such story speaks of a man who was hunting with his young son. As they approached a section of trees, a deep dark feeling of dread came over the man. A feeling of depression and anxiety then followed. The man communicated to his son his immediate discomfort, then fell to the ground and couldn't speak.

As the young boy sped off to get help for his father, he was grabbed by two arms that dropped down from the coverage of the leaves. The father, unable to move, lay and watched in horror as his son was shredded into pieces. Once the attack was over, and it was believed the creature was satisfied, the heaviness lifted from the man. He was able to get to his feet and stumbled to the closest village for refuge. He told of the horror he had witnessed, and warned all to stay away from the trees.

The Giant of Asebu

The Asebu Kingdom is believed to have been founded by a giant known as Asebu Amenfi, or Sabou. It is believed that he possessed spiritual powers that allowed him to perform tasks that an ordinary human could not do. It is also said he had a magical sword and possessed a mystical rod that he utilized in his battles, helping him conquer his enemies. The giant is said to have led an army that chased off the children of Israel during the Exodus. He was the chief commander. It is written that when his men or soldiers drowned, he could not return to pharaoh. Asebu Amenfi fled with his family. They then went further down to Benin City in Nigeria and finally settled around the coastal region of Southern Ghana.

Once Asebu arrived in the Southern territory of Ghana, he joined forces with a hunter known as Nana Adzekase. Nana then became the first chief of Moree. Asebu Amenfi had a brother named Farnyi Kwegya, who had great skill when it came to fishing, so he took advantage of the abundance of fish in the waters of the territory and became the first to be named chief fisherman.

The giant had a sister by the name of Amenfiwaa.

His sister was the only one in charge of preparing his meals. The food the giant consumed daily was corn. Due to his size, he had a large appetite. Amenfiwaa was always preparing food to appease her brother's hunger. It is said he could eat up to two acres of corn in a month's time.

Asebu was so large, he carried a bamboo home upon his head that housed his entire family, including his sister, who prepared the food for him as he traveled around. When he would stop to rest, he would place his hand on a rock and leave his handprints. His fingerprints upon the rocks are now said to be sacred, and the location is considered to be a heritage site and proof that Asebu did in fact exist and roam the territory of Ghana.

The Crocodiles of Paga

Crocodiles have roamed the earth for well over two hundred million years, outliving the dinosaurs. In the town of Paga, you'll find a sacred crocodile pond where the local people believe the crocodiles that reside in the waters hold the souls of the village's deceased. As a result, the animals are considered to be sacred to the locals. They claim that whenever any important individual in the village passes away, one of the sacred crocodiles will then pass shortly after. The pond is completely landlocked, and it is believed the oldest crocodiles in the water are close to one hundred years old.

Crocodiles are generally known to be extremely aggressive, but this is not the case in the small town of Paga. This town in northern Ghana has the most docile and tame of the entire predator species. The crocodiles swim alongside children while their fathers fish and their mothers wash clothes on the banks of the water. No one to date has ever been harmed by any of the crocodiles who dwell in the territory. Harming a crocodile is a capital offence in Paga. Harming or killing a crocodile is considered homicide in the eyes of the people.

The legend of the Paga Crocodile Pond dates back over six hundred years to a time at which it is said one of the crocodiles had led a young man to safety. Many generations ago, Paga was founded by an individual known as Patriarch Nave. Nave's grandfather Panlogo wanted the chief position overseeing the territory, but his brother was the one who won and was granted the position and title. Panlogo, so full of rage and disappointment, decided to leave the territory with his followers and those who supported him.

He headed north to the area of Tampela on the edge of Burkina Faso. Unfortunately, his enemies and the ones who opposed him and wanted his head followed him and his people. When Panlogo and his people came upon a raging river, they were unable to cross; it prevented their escape. There was no way to cross the river as far as they could see, and they had no means of transport or time to build a craft.

Soon desperation set in, and they believed they were about to meet their fate, when Panlogo spotted a crocodile in the water just a few yards from them. Panlogo and his people believed wholeheartedly that the spirits or souls of their ancestors did in fact reside within the crocodiles. Panlogo then pleaded to the crocodile for help and swore in gratitude that, from that time on, neither that crocodile nor any other will be ever hurt, killed, consumed, or be mistreated in anyway by his people. Panlogo and his people all took turns and climbed upon the crocodile's back and crossed the river to safety.

The Adze of Ghana

The Adze is a legend of the Ewe people of Ghana. Other names the Adze is known by is the African witch or Ghana vampire. There is a long-established belief that this vampiric type of creature is nocturnal and only goes out at night. The Adze is said to be able to transform itself into a firefly. Fireflies, as with other insects, can appear right in front of you without you noticing it's near. With that form, it is much easier for the Adze to attack a potential victim, and it would also allow the vampiric spirit to enter any believed-to-be-secure home through small entrances or openings such as crevices in the walls, keyholes, and any tiny gaps under doors. Once it has entered into the home, the real terror begins.

The Adze shapeshifts into this form deliberately, with full intent of evil and to not to be easily seen. The Ewe people believe that this vampiric spirit looks like what they define as a "corpse candle." Much like the corpse candles spoken of in Welsh and Irish folklore, the Adze can look like small balls of light from afar.

The people warn and caution not to attempt to capture one, as it will morph into human form. Once the Adze turns into its human appearance, it is said the creature will attack, mutilate, and eat the organs of animals and humans. The Ewe people also believe when the Adze is in its insect form, it will begin to suck out the blood of a human while they are sleeping, and spread numerous forms of disease. They believe this is a possible explanation for the malarial outbreaks in their country and other insect-borne diseases that plague the people.

It is believed by some that the Adze targets its victims based on age and gender. To them, the younger and more innocent, the better. So they prefer children, as the glow of their light is believed to lure children near or draw those who are unfortunate enough not to know the lore. But women and men do and will in fact fall victim as well. The unfortunate individual who the Adze targets is said to possibly become a witch, or will be possessed by the Adze's spirit once all the blood is drained. When possessed, the body is said to lurk within the shadows hunched over, staring ahead in a zombielike trance. Some also speak of the possessed body screaming, as if in excruciating pain. Legend goes on to state that there's no spell, potion, or weapon that can ward one off, and no real cure for the bitten.

11

Vietnam

Vietnam's first civilization began over five thousand years ago. But numerous tribes existed and flourished until around 207 BC, when their territory was taken over by a Chinese lord. This was when a kingdom was established known as Nam Viet. In 111 BC, Nam Viet then became part of a Chinese empire and oversaw the north territory until AD 939. In 939, a Vietnamese commander by the name of Ngo Quyen organized a revolt, or protest, that overtook and drove the Chinese out. Fast-forward to 1802, when a Nguyen lord renamed the country Vietnam.

In World War II, Japan took control briefly, and when the war ended in Japan's defeat in 1945, the leader Ho Chi Minh, of the Vietnamese Communist Party, announced and declared Vietnam an independent nation. In 1957, communist rebels in the southern territory known as Viet Cong came into power. Then war between the South and the North began. Soon other countries, such as Russia, the United States, and China, became involved. The fighting viciously continued until the year 1975. At this time the communists overran the south and took its capital, Saigon.

Vietnam is now a socialist state, run and governed by the Communist Party of Vietnam. A president who is chosen by the National Assembly is head of the state and commander of overseeing the armed forces. The prime minister is appointed by the president, who runs and oversees the government.

A large population of Vietnamese people live within the countryside, near the river delta regions. Most recently, people have started to migrate to the main cities of Hanoi and Ho Chi Minh, which was formerly Saigon. Vietnamese food is a blend of Thai and Chinese styles, which includes seafood, homegrown fruits, and vegetables.

Vietnam is a large contributor in the export of crude oil, rice, electronics, and coffee. Between 1975 and the late 1980s, Vietnam traded mainly with other communist countries, but since the collapse of the Soviet Union in 1990, it has expanded trade with other nations.

The mountainous terrain, forests, long coastlines, and wetlands of Vietnam contain many current habitats of wildlife. There are well over 270 different types of mammals, over 80 amphibians, over 800 species of birds, and 180 reptiles living in the area. There are also many rare animals that reside in the territory, such as the giant catfish, Sumatran rhinos, Indochinese tigers, and Saola antelopes. There are thirty government reserves and parks to help preserve and protect the animals. These territories are crucial for their survival, as much territory has been cleared to grow crops, build homes, and for lumber.

Vietnam at one time was covered with tropical forests, but in the last few hundred years, the increased activity involving logging projects has greatly reduced the forests' coverage. The government is working on launching different programs of replanting in an attempt to restore the woodlands.

―

Devil Creature of Son Doong Cave

There are tales told regarding strange creatures or monsters living and dwelling underground, in caves, and even in our homes. They are said to come up to steal our children, or wait until we wander close enough to grab us. A race of what many call reptilian people are encountered and reported each year all across the globe. Many of the eyewitnesses who have made reports of such an encounter, in most cases, are just ordinary folks who, until their eyes set sight on a reptilian, never believed. In many cases, these individuals still can't say "believe" is the correct word, as they just can't wrap their minds around the experience. What they saw was real, but how could it be? With so many sightings each year, one would believe that in many ways the reptilians present themselves on purpose, as if they want to be seen.

This seems to be the case when it comes to the Devil Creature of Son Doong Cave. In Vietnam, there is said to be a reptilian-like cryptid reported to have made its presence known and captured on camera in the Son Doong Cave. In 1992, a local man by the name of Ho-Khanh is believed to be the one who originally discovered the cave and encountered what he described as some sort of "devil creature." His description of this creature was as having a humanlike body, but with the skin and face that resembled that of a "dragon" or large lizard. He took a single photograph and allegedly unknowingly captured one of these creatures within the darkened area where he aimed the camera.

In 1970, in the South Vietnam territory, near the same connected cave system, an American military unit on patrol witnessed what they described as possibly two reptilian people or beings at the entrance of a cave. The creatures were said to be standing upright and around seven feet tall. They had scaly rough-looking skin that was dark in color. As the military unit approached, the figures turned and fled into the opening of the cave. The unit did not pursue, but moved on.

The Sơn Doong Cave is located near the Laos-Vietnam border and is said to be one of the largest known caves in the entire world. Year after year, locals who reside in the territory close to the Son Doong cave in Vietnam have reported strange events taking place, such as unexplained deaths and disappearances. Even stranger, many have claimed to have come across unusual reptilian abominations, such as humanlike snakes. Some believe these sightings correspond with disappearances, and what the people witnessed was a large snake either devouring a human or regurgitating one. Nevertheless, the people believe these are spawns of reptilian creatures believed to dwell down deep within the cave and have been said to kill those who venture too far within the cave's interior.

Since the cave was opened to the public, many who

have visited with no information of the area have submitted unsettling reports regarding witnessing what some describe as entity beings lurking in the shadows. In 2015 a video surfaced with what is allegedly claimed to be the "Devils of Soon Dong Cave." Many believe the legend, the picture, and the video to be a hoax, while others strongly disagree.

Batutut

The Batutut, also referred to as the Forest People, Vietnam War Ape, Wild Man, or Nguoi Rung, is said and believed to be a hominid cryptid very similar to the popular Sasquatch or Bigfoot creature reported across the globe. The Batutut is said to dwell in the Vu Quang nature reserve territory and many other areas of Vietnam. Reports claim the creature is extremely aggressive and will kill any human who dares to get too close. The Batutut is also known for charging, hollering, screaming, and famed for chasing.

The first recorded account of a Batutut was in 1918 when a hunter was out in the forest and came across some human footprints. The hunter came across the beast that was leaving the footprints. The hunter claimed to see the creature devour what looked to be a frog as it sat in a tree.

The Batutut is described by witnesses as being six to seven feet tall and covered with matted hair. The hair ranges in color per witness, as some gave account of gray, dark brown, and even black. Unlike most descriptions of a bipedal hairy man, the Batutut is said by many to have sections of the body that is just rough skin patches, such as the face, hands, and the soles of its feet. The creature walks bipedal upright on two legs, with the arms swinging side to side just above the creature's knees.

When war landed upon the territory, an Airborne Division team encountered what they believed to be a Batutut. It had a long, cone-shaped head, the face was covered in orange to red hair, and the eyes were black as night. As the creature stepped toward the team into a clearing, the team noticed the rest of its body was extremely muscular. After a short time, the creature turned and walked back into the thick forest.

As one would expect, there were numerous other sightings of large bipedal hairy creatures encountered by military teams while deep in the jungle. Half-man, half-beast, with dark eyes, a cone-like shaped head, long fangs, and a tail attached to their backside. Some soldiers reported that they had been attacked by humanoid creatures, which were dubbed the "Rock Apes." The name came from multiple teams claiming to have had rocks thrown at them. Some never saw the source of the incoming rocks, while others clearly witnessed the creatures tossing large boulder-sized rocks in their direction. These creatures left even the hardest of combat troops frightened and on their toes. The Rock Apes were said to be mostly active during dusk and into the night, and were reported to always travel in groups.

The Vietnamese Giant Centipede

The Vietnamese giant centipede, also known as the Chinese red-headed centipede, orange-legged centipede, Vietnamese centipede, and the jungle centipede. These large and extremely aggressive centipedes can be found throughout the Vietnam territory. Despite the name, this arthropod inhabits more than just Vietnam, but also dwells in other parts of the world. They can grow up to ten inches in length, while having well over twenty individual body sections, or segments. It can take the centipede up to three years to achieve its full growth. For an arthropod, it possesses a rather long lifespan and can live up to ten years.

Their method of attack is to go after any prey that they feel they're capable of overpowering, tightly coiling around it, and sinking their forcipules deep into the prey's flesh; it will then inject venom as is needed to kill. The powerful venom is located in two legs that are modified to inject from different angles. These legs are tipped on the ends with sharp claws attached to the glands that contain the venom. The forcipules sit on the top of the head. The head is protected by a flat shield guard and has two antennas. The eyesight of the centipede is believed to be extremely poor, but it guides itself well by using the chemoreceptors and antennas.

The effects of the venom on smaller animals such as bats, birds, and even medium-sized insects is said to cause paralysis, and death is swift. In humans, the venom can generate extreme pain, yet its toxin rarely causes life-threatening reactions. It can, however, lead to necrosis and cell decay. This particular species of centipede represents the only one to have a human fatality attributed to a bite, which is believed to have been to a severe allergic reaction.

The "CON RIT" of Vietnam

Sea creatures or lake monsters are a staple in the

world of cryptozoology. These aquatic, serpentine creatures have been reported across the globe for thousands
of years. The descriptions for some are very similar and
resemble those of other popular lake monsters such as
Nessie in Loch Ness and Champ in the waters of Lake
Champlain. Common descriptions include humped
backs and scaly skin, while others report smooth skin.
The heads have been described as snake or reptilian,
while others have mentioned a head that resembles that
of a horse.

Along the coast of northern Vietnam's Gulf of
Tonkin, one such creature has been reported. The
characteristics or description is not what one would
expect or have read about. This aquatic creature is
described as looking insect-like in appearance and has
been gifted the name the Serpent of Halong Bay, also
known as the Sea Dragon. The Halong Bay serpent is
said to have no fins and is large-bodied, long-necked, or
even crocodilian or prehistoric in its appearance. The
creature is said to have hundreds of legs and has a
painful venomous bite.

This creature in the Vietnamese language translates
to Con Rit, which is a term that stands for millipede.
This monster has been feared, and tales of encounters
have been passed down in Vietnamese folklore for
years. Some stories date back for centuries. However,

this cryptid's activities were reported to be at their peak during the nineteenth and twentieth centuries.

Many of the reports of this creature are by fearful individuals who claim they were attacked while fishing in their boats. Some boats are said to have been over-turned, and the helpless people were then devoured by the creature. There are also reports of large ships being attacked and overturned. While the sailors tried to flee to safety, they were pulled under the surface of the water, never to be seen again.

Lac-con-Quan, named the second king of Vietnam, set out to capture and kill the monster. It is reported that after the long search, the king and his crew captured, killed, and chopped up the beast into pieces. Legend tells that there are many odd-shaped stones that are believed to have been left by the king and his crew and are the pieces of the serpent. They can be seen on the shores of Halong Bay's Ca-Ba Island.

A young adult at the age of eighteen years old, by the name of Tran Van Con, claimed to have seen the carcass of one of the creatures. He claimed the crea-ture was missing its head, and the decomposing body was over fifty feet long and the width was between three to four feet wide. The body seemed to be in different segments or parts, with legs ranging from two to three feet long. The skin was dark gray, and the color covered it from head to tail. When others were notified of the carcass, it was no longer there. So no biological samples were ever taken. Still to this day, the whereabouts of the carcass remains a mystery.

It's been many years since the creature's last reported sighting. The lack of reports most likely means it has died off, giving way to its own extinction, or what many believed to be the creature was in fact not a creature at all.

Afterword

As an individual holding a lifelong love of monsters and the unexplained, I can only believe these subjects fascinate my inner being and imagination just as much as any mature adult or as an unexperienced, and curious adolescent. It would appear via conversations I have had with folks from all walks of life, age, and gender, my mindset speaks true to many. Simply just the mention of legends or monsters creates a spark in one's eye.

We live in a world in which our lives are subject to the monotonous, repetitive aspects of our visual surroundings and what we believe we know or understand. The everyday "norm" and a pursuit for public acceptance can have a debilitating effect on one's ability to open their mind, initiate imagination, and accept what they do not understand.

What is real…?

Bibliography

- Accessgenealogy (2020)
- All About History (2002–2018)
- Bailey, Col., *Shadow of the Thylacine* (Mike Press 2013)
- Department of History, Front Ehistory (2018–2019)
- Education Commission of the States (2018–2019)
- Fact Monster (2000–2019)
- Godfrey, Linda, *American Monsters*, Penguin, (2014)
- History, *Famous Inventors*, ThoughtCo (2019)
- Holiday, FW, *The Great Orm of Loch Ness* (Faber & Faber, 1968)

- Landsburg, Alan, *In search of Myths and Monsters* (Corgi, 1977)
- Course Daily (2019 updated)
- Native American, Indigenous People, Encyclopedia Britannica (2000 to 2019)
- Overview Native Americans, Scholastic (2016)
- Office of the Historian, US Department of State (2019)
- Rock on the Net (1997 to 2019)
- *Scientific American* (2017)
- Sykes, Bryan, *Nature of the Beast* (Coronet, 2015)
- Info Please (2019)

*Some cases not specific enough to reference.

About the Author

Kenney W. Irish AKA "The Cryptopunkologist," is an author, hardcore/punk musician and sales/marketing professional. Originally from the northern parts of Vermont, he recently re-located to the beautiful Adirondacks area of upstate New York. He's had a love of folklore, legends, monsters, and U.F.O stories his entire life and turned that passion into books, speaking engagements, television and co-hosting a radio show. For more information visit him at www. kwirish.com

Also by Kenney W. Irish

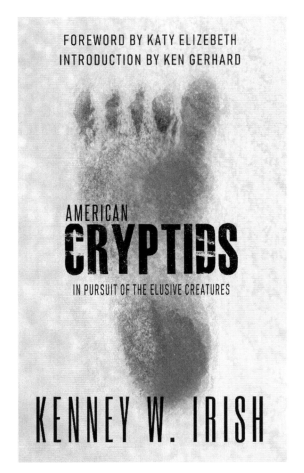

FOREWORD BY KATY ELIZEBETH
INTRODUCTION BY KEN GERHARD

AMERICAN
CRYPTIDS
IN PURSUIT OF THE ELUSIVE CREATURES

KENNEY W. IRISH

American Cryptids: In Pursuit of The
Elusive Creatures

Printed in Great Britain
by Amazon

11047134R00087